LACONICS
OF
LIBERTY

Short Passages and Poems from the Writings of Early Libertarians

Compiled by Charles T. Sprading
Annotated by Rob Weir

ANTIC PRESS
DOVER, NEW HAMPSHIRE

Antic Press
106 Court St.
Dover, NH 03820
www.anticpress.com

Laconics of Liberty/ Charles T. Sprading, Rob Weir. —1st ed.
ISBN 978-1-7338971-0-5

Contents

Foreword

A Lost Literature

How many proponents of liberty can you name who were active in the half-century between the American Civil War and World War One? How many of their works can you name? How many can you quote from?

If you are like most, this period draws a blank. But, in fact, this was a time of great optimism for liberty, when many liberal (in the original sense) thinkers and writers were active. There was a grand tradition of pamphleteers, editors, journalists, circuit speakers, book authors, essayists, humorists and poets who championed the cause of liberty before the calamity of the Great War and the subsequent rise of fascism.

Although some of this material was scholarly, much of it was written for, and appealed to, the average reader, appearing in periodicals like *Lucifer the Lightbearer*, *Blue-Grass Blade*, *Reedy's Mirror* and *Mother Earth*.

The proponents of liberty were a diverse lot. They called themselves anarchists (of various flavors), socialists, labor activists, mutualists, voluntaryists, Georgists, syndicalists, free thinkers, free speech activists, abolitionists, liberals, social reformers, secularists, anti-imperialists and other assorted radicals.

The Great Libertarians

To Charles T. Sprading (1871-1959), it was all good. Sprading was a political radical active in Los Angeles in the first decades of the 20th century, as president of the Liberal Club there, and founder of the Libertarian League. He published a dozen books over his long writing career, but one in particular stands out, his 1913 anthology, *Liberty and the Great Libertarians: An Anthology on Liberty, A Hand-Book of Freedom.* In this work he brought together chapter-length essays and excerpts from longer works, from a wide range of traditions: classical liberal, radical liberal and anarchist. (Noticeably absent is representation from Marxist writers. Sprading was very much in the Tuckerite camp, a pro-liberty anarchist, opposed to the authoritarianism of state socialism.)

These are not all *libertarian* in our modern sense of the term. Far from it. It is more of a first-cut of libertarianism, a philosophy of liberty forged in a world where primitive economic notations still prevailed, before the Marginalist Revolution in economics. Nevertheless, there is something in *Liberty and the Great Libertarians* for almost anyone to enjoy, whether right-libertarian or left-libertarian, whether anarcho-capitalist or anarcho-communist. It is also true, however, that there is much here to disagree with.

So, why did Sprading include so many diverse writers, expressing such opposing views? As he explains in his introduction:

> It will also be observed that extremes meet here and are equally provided for by liberty. The Individualist and the Communist, each advocating his own ideas, are both within the scope of equal liberty, and there is no conflict between them when the principle of liberty is adhered to; that is, if they produce and distribute among themselves. Plans voluntarily accepted by individuals or groups of individuals and not forced upon others are in no way a violation of liberty. They would be if others were forced to do so by the seizure of "all means of production and distribution," as the State Socialists purpose to do, thereby excluding non-conformers from their use. It is not the difference in taste between individuals that Libertarians object to, but the forcing of one's tastes upon another. Individualists believe in common ownership of such things as roads, streets and waterways, and Communists believe in individual ownership of such things as clothes and personal effects. They really merge into one another; but there is no need for either to conform to the other's taste or to be deprived of its own liberty.

In other words, although such views might contradict each other in the mind of a single person, they can coexist in the same world, provided they are pursued peacefully.

These Excerpts

At more than 500 pages in length, Sprading's full text for *Liberty and the Great Libertarians* requires quite a commitment. To whet the reader's appetite, I've excerpted and annotated a selection of the shorter items from Sprading's anthology, the aphorisms, short passages, poems, etc. Sprading called these the "Laconics of Liberty." (A laconic is a short, pithy saying. The citizens of ancient Sparta (*Lakedaímōn* in Greek) were reputed to be short on words, long on deeds.)

This is the message of liberty in its most distilled form. Short items like these commonly appeared in the activist newspapers of the day, in trade union journals and in pamphlets. Where today we post memes on Facebook, in those days they printed lines, like those that follow, in their publications.

I hope you will enjoy this short read, and gain a greater appreciation for an older, messier tradition of libertarian thought. Please enjoy these choicest pearls from the lost literature of liberty!

Rob Weir
Dover, New Hampshire.
March 2019

Editorial Remarks

I have aimed to keep Sprading's text intact, wherever reasonable. In only a small number of cases have I silently corrected minor errors or made minor formatting changes. I have not corrected variations in spelling in his source material, such as American versus English conventions. I have made no attempt to correct his loose use of punctuation.

I have added many annotations to Sprading's text, to make long-forgotten names and events more relatable to the reader of today. Along with the briefest possible biographical sketch, I've attempted to trace each quotation back to its original source, and verify it, using digital book and newspaper archives.

In some cases, my research revealed misquotations or even misattributions. Those are noted in footnotes. In a small number of cases I was able to identify neither the author nor the work. These may have been relatively minor local figures, in Sprading's circle in Los Angeles.

In several cases, Sprading gives us text that was assembled from non-contiguous paragraphs from a source work, or even from different source works. I've noted this discontinuity as […] (single work) or [….] (different works). Where multiple works were involved, I also explain in the footnote.

All the footnotes, and any errors contained therein, are my responsibility.

Introduction

[This is Charles T. Sprading's original introduction to his 1913 *Liberty and the Great Libertarians*, lightly annotated.]

The history of civilized man is the history of the incessant conflict between liberty and authority. Each victory for liberty marked a new step in the world's progress; so we can measure the advance of civilization by the amount of freedom acquired by human institutions.

The first great struggle for liberty was in the realm of thought. The Libertarians reasoned that freedom of thought would be good for mankind; it would promote knowledge, and increased knowledge would advance civilization. But the Authoritarians protested that freedom of thought would be dangerous; that people would think wrong; that a few were divinely appointed to think for the people, that these had books which contained the whole truth, and that further search was unnecessary and forbidden. The powers of Church and State were arrayed against the Libertarians; but, after the sacrifice of many great men, freedom in thought was won.

The second momentous contest was for the liberty to speak. The enemies of liberty, those possessing power and privilege, opposed freedom of speech, just as they had opposed freedom of thought. The Church said it was perilous to permit people to speak their minds;—they might speak the truth. The State said free speech was dangerous; it was not the duty of citizens to think and speak, but to obey. After much persecution the Libertarians were victorious, although such authoritarian institutions as the Catholic Church and the Spanish and Russian States do not even now concede freedom of thought and speech.

The third contest was for liberty of the press. The same old enemies who had so much to conceal opposed it, and their repressive measures added a long list of martyrs to the cause of freedom. Like free thought and free speech, free press has proved to be a powerful factor in human progress. It still has its enemies as of old, but their number and influence are dwindling.

The fourth struggle was for the liberty of assembly. Here again Libertarians met the same old enemies using the same old arguments. The people could not be permitted to assemble freely because they might come together and discuss matters relating to Church or State or plan treason and revolution. But again liberty was victorious, and free assembly has been found to be beneficial to the people, if not to some institutions.

The fifth important contest for liberty was in the field of religion. The Libertarians argued that freedom was as necessary and desirable in religion as in other human relations; that man should be free to worship at any shrine he pleased, or at no shrine; to worship as his reason and conscience dictated, or even not to worship at all. An infallible church could never permit fallible human beings to choose their own religion, but a succession of conflicts opened the gates of religious liberty.

In these five important spheres of human action there have been, against a sea of ignorance and tradition, five great victories for freedom. Liberty, wherever applied, has proved a benefit to the race;[1] furthermore, the most important steps in human progress would have been impossible without it; and if civilization is to advance, that advance can come only as a result of a broader and more complete freedom in all human relations. A principle that has proved its workability in five such important and vital phases of social evolution should prove desirable in all the affairs of man.

And here is the difference between the Libertarians and the Authoritarians: the latter have no confidence in liberty; they believe in compelling people to be good, assuming that people are totally depraved; the former believe in letting people be good, and maintain that humanity grows better and better as

---

[1] In Sprading's use, the term "the race" is synonymous with "the people." We should avoid reading our contemporary fraught meaning into an early 20th century text.

it gains more and more liberty. If Libertarians were merely to ask that liberty be tried in any one of the other fields of human expression they would meet the same opposition as their pioneer predecessors; but such is their confidence in the advantages of liberty that they demand, not that it be tried in one more instance only, but that it be universally adopted.[2]

Their demand is for equal liberty, which denies all privileges and permits no other restrictions than those imposed by social conditions. As it is their relation to their fellowmen with which they are concerned, Libertarians seek to promote equal liberty, and not absolute liberty. "Absolute liberty" means that liberty which disregards the liberty of others.[3] Some extreme individualists like Nietzsche believe in it; but absolute liberty, as the word implies, is unsocial, because it is unrelated. If there is an absolute, it is not a social law, for all social laws are relative. Equal liberty is bounded by the like liberty of all.[4]

Mere equality does not imply equal liberty, however, for slaves are equal in their slavery. Equal opportunity to rob others is not equal liberty, but its violation; it abridges "liberty to possess," and the "liberty to produce and to own the product." These liberties are implied by equality of liberty, just as equal opportunity is; equal robbery or equal slavery have no relation to equal liberty, but are its opposite. There are but two positions from which to choose, equal liberty or unequal liberty. Most persons believe in liberty for themselves, but not for others. Some Christians believe in hell for others, but not for themselves. Libertarians are not like either, for they demand the same liberty for others that they ask for themselves.

Its enemies deride liberty as an abstraction. It is abstract, but so are most of the sciences. Mathematics, for instance, is abstract, but we find that this abstraction

---

[2] Libertarianism takes a good idea, liberty, a principle nearly all agree with, and applies it consistently and to its logical conclusion.

[3] One of many such oppositions which could be suggested: justice vs. social justice, negative rights vs. positive rights, equality of opportunity vs. equality of outcome, etc. In each pair, libertarians support the former, authoritarians the latter.

[4] This is the Law of Equal Liberty, articulated by Herbert Spencer (*Social Statics*, 1851): "...that every man may claim the fullest liberty to exercise his faculties compatible with the possession of like liberty to every other man."

fits every concrete fact in the universe. So it is with abstract liberty. It will fit every concrete social fact; it will solve every social ill.

Liberty has its positive and its negative side—it negates authority and tyranny, but it affirms equity and justice; that is, it negates the bad and affirms the good. Destruction is necessary, but construction is equally so; it is essential to tear away the old building in order to erect the new in its place, but before consenting to its demolition the occupant may demand to know what is to take its place, and the architect should furnish him specifications of the proposed structure. There are those who are most successful in tearing down the old building, who, however, may not have the abstract idea of the new structure in their minds, while there are others who excel in building up the new. Both are essential. It is absurd to say that clearing the ground is sufficient, for tomorrow's weeds will grow where they are cleared today. How often is one superstition overthrown only to be replaced by a different one! Truth must be substituted for error,—and this is the work of the positive side of liberty. Liberty means freedom to construct the new as well as freedom to destroy the old. A society of Libertarians will destroy the old, but they will also build the new, and whatever ground they clear of weeds will be sown with seeds of progress.

Rights

The word "Right" has many meanings; and unfortunately it has two contradictory ones—legal rights and ethical right—that lead to much confusion of thought. Legal rights are:

- "Any power or privilege vested in a person by the law"

- "A claim or title to or interest in anything whatsoever that is enforceable by law"

- "A franchise—a specific right or privilege granted or established by governmental authority"

- "A capacity or privilege the enjoyment of which is secured to a person by law, hence the interest or share which anyone has in a piece of property, title, claim, interest"

It will be seen from these accepted definitions that legal right is synonymous with power; whoever or whatsoever has the power, has the right. Now, governments have most power, therefore have most rights. If individuals have any legal rights, it is because governments have granted them in the way of "franchise," "title," "privilege," etc. Legal right means to take, to have and to hold. There is no sentiment in legal right; it is the offspring of power only—"Might is right!"

Right in its ethical sense is defined thus:

- "Right is in accordance with equity"
- "Conformity to the standard of justice"
- "Right is identical with the good, not deviating from the true and just"
- "Freedom from guilt"

A comparison of these two conceptions of right will disclose the fundamental disagreement between them. Although the legal and ethical definitions of right are the antithesis of each other, most writers use them as synonyms. They confuse power with goodness, and mistake law for justice.

Ethical right is largely abstract; legal right is mostly concrete. Ethical right the just man wishes to be established; legal right is already established. Ethical right and legal right mutually exclude each other; where one prevails, the other cannot endure. One is founded on power, on might; the other on justice, on equality. One appeals to the sword to settle matters, the other appeals to the judgment of men. For illustration: Governments have the right to do wrong; that is, they have the power, the legal right, to do anything they choose, regardless of whether it is good or bad—and their choice is usually bad from the ethical standpoint. Governments can and do invade nations, rob the people of their property, enslave or kill the inhabitants; all in perfect accord with legal rights, but in gross violation of ethical right. Let it be understood that the right of a government is coextensive with its power; it has not the right to invade, enslave or kill the people of a stronger nation or government, for it lacks the power on which this right is based; but, having the power, it has the right to commit these acts against a weaker nation. Let us not mistake things as they are for things as they ought to be.

It is absurd to speak of the slave having the "right" to liberty. It is a curious sort of right that could in no way be exercised during the thousands of years in which slavery existed; surely not a legal right, for slavery was legal then. Neither had the slave an ethical right; for ethical right means "justice," "equity," "liberty," the very things he did not have: it is even doubtful if many of the slaves had the least idea of justice and liberty. It is only correct to say that they should have had such a right. To say they had it, is like saying one already has a fortune that he is hoping to acquire.[5]

Justice

Some of the accepted definitions of Justice are:

- "Conformity to truth, fact or right reason; fairness; rightfulness; truth; impartiality;"

- "The rendering to everyone his due or right; just treatment;"

- "To do justice to; to treat with fairness or according to merit; to render what is due to;"

- "Rightfulness; uprightness; equitableness, as the justice of a cause."

These definitions are accepted by Libertarians, who believe that justice is that which ought to be done by one to another. But what is the true criterion of the conduct we expect from another? How are we to know it is just? By what standard is justice to be judged? Authorities on law answer, "Custom": whatever is customary is just. Therefore, the lawyer looks for "precedents." No lawyer will declare, "My client broke this law, and he did right, for it is a bad law": that would be in violation of custom and precedent, and he dare not say it; but he will ransack the maze of law for a precedent—and will find one, too!

---

[5] Sprading neglects to mention that there can also be claims that arise out of voluntary transactions. If you and I bargain that, in return for two loaves of bread today, you will give me a dozen eggs by next week, I then have a claim on those eggs, and you have an obligation to provide them. Even without government enforcement of such a contract, the obligation has moral, and perhaps even social weight. So, the thing that distinguishes legal and ethical rights is not really the presence of claims, but whether those claims originated via a just process, e.g., via a consensual agreement.

To quote only one of the great authorities on law: James Coolidge Carter in his *Law: Its Origin, Growth and Function*, page 163,[6] says, "Justice consists in the compliance with custom in all matters of difference between men," and he tells us on the same page that "This accords with the definition of the Roman law." But custom and precedent are defective as a basis for that conception of justice which recognizes good acts only; for custom and precedent can be found for all kinds of acts, good, bad and indifferent. Some of our savage ancestors had the habit, or "custom," of eating their dead parents; so, by proving the precedent or custom, we can prove that cannibalism is just! Custom may suffice as the basis of law but is inadequate as the basis of justice. Tyranny, not liberty, has been the custom in the past; and so Libertarians reject custom as a guiding principle, just as they reject power or might. They know that justice is not something that was, or is, but that is to be. Pascal saw the absurdity of law and justice that have their source in custom, for he says: "In the just and unjust we find hardly anything which does not change its character in changing its climate. Three degrees of elevation of the pole reverse the whole of jurisprudence. A meridian is decisive of truth, or a few years of possession. Fundamental laws change! Right has its epochs! A pleasant justice that, which a river or a mountain limits! Truth on this side the Pyrenees, error on the other!"[7]

And who can know what the law really is? In the United States we have over 50,000 laws, most of which conflict with each other, and to interpret them we employ an army of lawyers and judges, who disagree as to the intent or applicability of every law. The writers on the theory of law are equally perplexed. Sir Henry Maine says: "There is much widespread dissatisfaction with existing theories of jurisprudence, and so general a conviction that they do not really solve the questions they pretend to dispose of, as to justify the suspicion that some line of inquiry necessary to a perfect result has been incompletely followed or altogether omitted by their authors." Perceiving, like Sir Henry Maine and other honest writers on law and justice, the "widespread dissatisfaction with existing theories of jurisprudence," Libertarians reject them altogether as the basis of justice.

---

[6] James Coolidge Carter, *Law: Its Origin Growth and Function* (New York: G.P. Putnam's Sons, 1907); Available online: https://archive.org/details/lawitsorigingrow00cartuof
[7] Blaise Pascal, *Pensées* (1660), Section V, 294.

Law

Some writers on this subject have made justice the basis of law, while others have made law the basis of justice; but, as a matter of fact, statute law did not have its source in justice nor is justice the outcome of such law. Lawmakers are not imbued with the idea of arriving at justice. The motive most prevalent among them is that of personal or class benefit, benefit to the makers of law or to the makers of the lawmakers. Benefit to them means property-getting. They find that the State is of great assistance both in this property-getting and in the property-holding part of the game, so they seize the State and use it as their instrument in acquiring and defending property. These lawmakers believe that the law should reflect their interests; and as they enact nearly all laws they see to it that the law represents their desires and not the ideas of equity.[8]

If all men had the same interests, there would be less harm in permitting a part of the people to legislate for all; but this is not the case. There is a great conflict of interests between the possessed and the dispossessed, between the poor and the rich, between the weak and the strong, between the ruler and the ruled, between the worker and the shirker, between the producer and the appropriator, which is apparent in existing laws, always made by those powerful enough to take advantage of the State and of the law-abiding sentiment of the people.[9] That their laws conflict with justice is no concern of theirs, for profit and not justice is their object. The object is legitimate because they make it legitimate. The game they play is lawful because they make the law to uphold their game; but they raise a hue and cry for "law and order" if they find any game conflicting with theirs, and declare it unlawful. It is easy to see that laws thus enacted are unjust, for to be just a law must be enacted for the benefit of all; thus it is in no wise logical to presume that the "legal" is the just.

---

[8] A precursor of "public choice" thinking, treating government decision-making as a market activity and subjecting it to economic analysis. Who benefits from a monopoly as a lawgiver?

[9] This more pessimistic view should be contrasted with the classical liberal perspective, from Adam Smith to Bastiat to Mises, of the "harmony of the rightly understood interests of all members of the market society." (Mises, *Human Action*, chapter 25.)

When we compare the laws made today and the method and purpose of their making, with those of the past, we find them to be in perfect harmony. It was the law and custom of the past to provide for a class of idlers, it was customary for the powerful to enslave the weak, for the rich to rob the poor, for the unscrupulous to make laws in their own interests, even as it is the law and custom today. Surely it must be evident that law does not have its basis in justice, but rather in custom. To both law and custom, justice is a total stranger.

When we know the source of law, we cease to wonder at the conduct of those who accept law as a guiding principle; we understand why they conduct themselves so badly from the standpoint of justice and still keep out of jail; we also understand why some who have violated no rule of justice go to jail. Most people accept law as their guide to conduct; they find it to be more profitable than following the rules of justice. They are always asking, "What is the law?" "Can I do that and not be arrested?" To them anything within the law is right; yet we know that the greatest injustices are committed within the law. They would see nothing wrong in murder, if it was lawful; but murder is lawful only to the makers of law, to the State or the Government, which indulges its own murderous inclinations, legitimately, by capital punishment and by war.

Equal Liberty

The Law of Equal Liberty is the principle that is offered by Libertarians as a substitute for these conflicting and unjust customs of the past. This law has been well formulated by that great philosopher and sociologist, Herbert Spencer. Here it is in brief: "That every man may claim the fullest liberty to exercise his faculties compatible with the possession of like liberty by every other man."[10] This gives us a basis for justice in perfect harmony with the idea of equity. Equal liberty is the essence of equity, and is not equity just? If there are to be laws in a free society, they must be based upon equal liberty or they will be unjust.

---

[10] *Social Statics* (1851)

Natural Law and Statute Law

Some authorities on law hold that statute law is based on natural law and therefore in perfect harmony with it, but this will not bear analysis. The natural law of evolution, of development, is variation, differentiation; statute law is intended to produce similarity and uniformity. The first depends upon dynamic forces, the second upon customs of the dead. The first is the law of the new; the second, the law of the old. The first does its own enforcing; the second needs to be enforced. The first cannot be suspended; the second is changed to suit the lawmakers. The law of variation has guided us in the path of progression, while statute law has tended only toward retrogression.

In the animal world, when the law of variation produces an animal differing somewhat from its kind, whether it be in different physical characteristics, to more perfectly adapt it to its environment, or in the addition of new organs to adapt it to a different environment, it is permitted by others of its species to live and propagate its kind, and often produces an entirely new and higher type of animal. But how do upholders of statute law act toward those who differ from them? Let the treatment accorded a Jesus, a Bruno, a Ferrer, be the answer.[11] Statute law is not based on natural law; they are the antithesis of each other.

Government

The greatest violator of the principle of equal liberty is the State. Its functions are to control, to rule, to dictate, to regulate, and in exercising these functions it interferes with and injures individuals who have done no wrong. The objection to government is, not that it controls those who invade the liberty of others, but that it controls the non-invader. It may be necessary to govern one who will not govern himself, but that in no wise justifies governing one who is capable of and willing to govern himself. To argue that because some need restraint all must be restrained is neither consistent nor logical.

---

[11] Jesus, of course, needs no introduction. Giordano Bruno (1548-1600) was a Dominican friar who was burned at the stake by the Inquisition in Rome for his heretical cosmological theories. Francisco Ferrer Guardia (1859-1909) was a free-thinker and founder of the progressive *Escuela Moderna* (Modern School), a series of secular working-class schools in Catalonia. He was executed by firing squad in Barcelona.

Governments cannot accept liberty as their fundamental basis for justice, because governments rest upon authority and not upon liberty. To accept liberty as the fundamental basis is to discard authority; that is, to discard government itself; as this would mean the dethronement of the leaders of government, we can expect only those who have no economic compromise to make to accept equal liberty as the basis of justice.

If a person accepts the standard of might or power as the correct guiding principle, as the State does, then he can have no reasonable complaint against the unjust conditions that prevail, for they are the logical outcome of the existing principle of government. One must not complain against powerful corporations, for they are the acme of power; by the power of the State they have been granted special "privileges," such as franchises, large land grants, the use and control of public utilities, etc., all of which add to their power by adding to their wealth. In order to oppose logically this inequitable condition, it is necessary to adopt a different standard from that of might or power.

It is the nature of government to invade. It will impose itself upon the non-invasive individual as readily as it will upon the invasive one. It will seize his property through taxation, or otherwise, and use it for purposes of which the individual does not approve—for going to war, for instance, or building warships (things obnoxious to the peaceful man). It makes so many complicated laws that the individual is bound to break some of them. There are innumerable laws on our statute books, and no lawyer or judge pretends that he knows ten per cent of them; yet the layman may be held to a strict obedience of any or all of them, and if he pleads that he did not know the law he is told that ignorance of the law is no excuse for its breach. He is supposed to know ninety per cent more of law than its students, practitioners, and makers. The more laws, the more ignorance of them; the more ignorance of the law, the more the laws are broken; the more the laws are broken, the more criminals there are; and the more criminals, the more policemen, detectives, lawyers, judges, and other officials that go to make up a strong and expensive government. All of this is good for government officials, but bad for the citizens who carry the load.

Rulers have always profited by the mistakes of individuals, and have always made conditions such that mistakes were unavoidable.[12]

The State is even more unfair than the law it pretends to enforce. It never enforces the law equitably, but always favors the rich and the powerful. When it so happens that the law conflicts with the interests of the powerful, it is invariably interpreted in their favor.

The protective part of government is greatly exaggerated. It collects taxes on the theory that it renders an equivalent in protection, but if a crime is committed and a poor man is accused, instead of protecting him, it turns all of its machinery against him; instead of presenting both sides, so that justice may be arrived at, it presents one side and leaves it to the unfortunate one to present the other side if he can.[13] It suppresses all evidence in its possession favorable to the individual, and conceals all evidence against him until the day of trial and then presents it: and all under the pretense of protecting the individual! The fact is, the government is a prosecutor and not a defender; it is an invader and not a protector.

The Libertarians say: Let those who believe in religion have religion; let those who believe in government, have government; but also let those who believe in liberty, have liberty, and do not compel them to accept a religion or a government they do not want. It is as unjust to force one's government upon another, as it is unjust to force one's religion upon another. This was done in the past; but we have won religious freedom, and must now work toward political freedom. We no longer believe that it is just for one man to govern two men, but we have yet to outgrow the absurd belief that it is just for two men to govern one man. To govern a man—that is, to control him, to dictate to him, to rule him—is to violate the principle of equal liberty, for there is the same inequality between the governor and the governed, between the dictator and those dictated to, between the ruler and the ruled, that there was between the master and his

---

[12] This is quite a prescient critique of how Big Government leads to an explosion of crimes. A more modern treatment of this theme is Harvey Silverglate, *Three Felonies A Day: How the Feds Target the Innocent* (New York: Encounter Books, 2011).

[13] Note that this was written well before the U.S. Supreme Court, in *Gideon v. Wainwright* (1963), held that counsel must be provided for defendants who would otherwise be unable to afford a defense attorney.

slave. The power to command and the weakness to obey are the essence of government and the quintessence of slavery.

It is not even just to restrain the invader, but it seems expedient to do so, since he fails to restrain himself. He has violated the principles of justice and liberty, but we are doing likewise when we take his liberty from him. However, it seems necessary to do so for self-protection against an invader who will not recognize the principle of equal liberty. It is like going to war in self-defense: it is not just, but it may be expedient to do so. It is not just, because war of any kind is not just; but in the extreme alternative of going to war or being exterminated, we will choose the lesser of the two evils. So if we are compelled to restrain the invader to prevent invasive acts, why not be honest and admit that it is a bad state of affairs which necessitates it, and one to be dispensed with just as soon as the invader is cured? The principle of equal liberty, which implies equal opportunity, will cure all but the insane.[14]

Humane men look forward to the day when all of the aggressive and violent parts of the government will cease and only the defensive part remain. "But," say men like Tucker,[15] "that will be the end of government." Very well, let what he calls government go. "But how will you abolish it?" will be asked. It may be answered by asking another: How was slavery abolished? Was it abolished by all the people going into the slave-owning business? Certainly not. It was abolished because the people disliked it and opposed it; because they would not support the business and the people in the business. So it will be with government, or that part of it that is not protective, but invasive; when the people withdraw their support from it, when they oppose it and refuse to pay taxes, when they refuse to go to war, refuse to accept office to enforce unjust laws, then the end will come, and a voluntary co-operative society of free people will take its place, and nothing of the invasive nature of the State will remain.

---

[14] Of course, today most libertarians would argue that self-defense is both just and expedient, that this is true even according to the principle of equal liberty. However, there is a pacifist school of libertarianism. Its most notable proponent was Robert LeFevre (1911-1986), who emphasized prevention of crimes but disclaimed the use of violence to counter violence.

[15] Benjamin Tucker (1854-1939), American individualist anarchist, early publisher of a 19th century anarchist magazine, *Liberty*.

Crimes and Criminals

Most crimes are offenses against property. The struggle for property leads to depredations and infractions of the principles of equal liberty in various ways. Greed on the one side and poverty on the other, is the cause of so-called crime. To cure crime, it is necessary to remove its cause. The disease of greed may not be curable, but its baneful results can be obviated by destroying special privileges, out of which ensues poverty, that in turn breeds crime.

Economists are agreed that there are four methods by which wealth is acquired by those who do not produce it. These are, interest, profit, rent and taxes, each of which is based upon special privilege, and all are gross violations of the principle of equal liberty.

First, Interest arises from the special privilege granting to a favored few, known as national bankers, the exclusive right of issuing money. The liberty to establish mutual banks or other free systems of issuing money would abolish interest.[16]

Second, Profits arise from such special privileges as copyrights, patent rights, franchises, grants, etc., all of which violate the principle of equal liberty.

Third, Rent arises from the special privilege of land titles, land grants, the right by deed to hold land and compel others to pay for its use. Equal liberty to use land would eliminate rent.

Fourth, Taxation is a special privilege assumed by the ruling class to levy tribute on their subjects, and is a violation of the liberty of those who do not want a ruling class.

Thus it is seen that the four methods of acquiring wealth and producing poverty rest upon special privileges granted by government. Thus government, producing the criminal rich and the criminal poor, is itself the cause of crime, and not its prevention, as stupid people believe. In order to perpetuate itself government must manufacture criminals; it rests on their backs and without them it would fall. If there were no criminals there would be no policemen, no

---

[16] Although economists in Austria, like Eugen von Böhm-Bawerk, had rigorously explained the origin of money interest, these German-language writings had yet achieved broader influence. Sprader, like many of his contemporary radicals, was mislead by his reliance on what would ultimately be seen as unworkable economic theories.

detectives, no lawyers, no judges, no courts, no legislatures, no penitentiaries—
no government, in fact. Government would cease without "criminals" to sustain
it, and to expect the government to remove its own foundation is idle.

If the cause of crime is removed it will be by Libertarians and not by
Authoritarians. It will be by those who hate it, not by those who profit by it.

Majority Rule

Majority rule, like every other rule, is a violation of the principle of equal
liberty. Like all other rules it rests on power. This power is the power of numbers; not the power of extermination by means of the bullet and the war club,
as in ages past, but of the same nature, having neither regard for justice nor
for reason. For centuries the only means at the disposal of power by which it
might acquire its ends was the bullet. All its conquest, its means of securing
the subserviency and exploitation of the weak, was by the method of extermination—the bullet. But, finally, the observation that a large army could conquer a small one led to the method of enumeration to settle a dispute instead
of the old one of extermination: the ballot instead of the bullet.[17] The ballot
is more economical of human life—but to use enumeration as the means of
arriving at justice is a poor substitute for reason.

A reasonable action on the part of the majority is very rare, while the evidence
of mob stupidity and brutality is overwhelming. The majority in power make
laws for their own financial benefit, disregarding the interests of the minority,
and when the weak minority, by adding to its numbers, becomes powerful, it, in
turn, does the same thing; thus, by appealing to power to settle their conflicting
interests, the conflict would go on forever.

Does it not seem a vast waste of valuable human material that the pioneers of
thought, those who by their genius dare to clear unknown paths in the arts and
sciences and in government, should have to conform to the dictates of that non-

---

[17] The imagined history of some ancient encounter between two vying factions of
society, where the antagonists met in the field of battle for some violent encounter,
and one side, seeing itself so vastly outnumbered, yielded to the more powerful party,
granting him victory without bloodshed. The implication is that any voting procure
partakes of at least the threat of violence. Voting is sublimated warfare.

creative, slow-moving mass, the majority? An appeal to the majority is a resort to force and not an appeal to intelligence; the majority is always ignorant, and by increasing the majority we multiply ignorance. The majority is incapable of initiative, its attitude being one of opposition toward everything that is new. If it had been left to the majority, the world would never have had the steamboat, the railroad, the telegraph, or any of the conveniences of modern life.

We are required to accept the decision of the majority as final, although the majority does and always has decided against the very things which have proved themselves most useful to society. In fact, every advance in civilization—in the arts, in language, in science, in invention and discovery—has been achieved, not because of the wish of the majority, but by the constant work and urgent demands of a persistent few. It took Voltaire and others of his kind half a century to convince the majority that it was being robbed and enslaved; and when a part of that majority was at last convinced, it did not use the educational method that had convinced them, but resorted to force to convince the rest. War, not logic, is the method of the mob.

If majority rule is right, then we have no just complaint to make against existing conditions, for the majority favors them or it surely would change them. The majority looks to its politicians for guidance. The successful politicians never advance new ideas, knowing that they must stay by the majority, echoing only the sentiment of the majority, or they will lose their jobs. The real educator does his work at his own expense, sows the seed, builds up a movement, perhaps; the politician snatches his idea and reaps the harvest, loudly declaring himself the author of the idea, and the majority accepts his assertion and follows him.

A political convention illustrates the workings of majority rule: If the minority in a party advocate a progressive move which is defeated when put to a vote in the convention, the minority are prohibited from advancing it during the campaign; if this minority refuse to advocate what the convention has decided to be right, they are barred from the platform and press, the cry of majority rule is raised against them, and they are called "traitors to the party;" but if they abandon their progressive ideas and advocate the wishes of the majority they are rewarded with office. Thus majority rule develops the dishonest politician: in order to rule sometime, he consents to being ruled at other times. The desire to rule and the willingness to be ruled ends in degradation; and no one who accepts the principles of equal liberty can indorse majority rule.

War

War is a violation of the principle of liberty as well as of justice. It is founded on force; its method is violence; its theory is "Might is right;" its purpose is to conquer or destroy. Its greatest heroes are those who have slaughtered the greatest number of people; its Alexanders, its Napoleons. Napoleon said that "God is always on the side of the strong battalions." When differences between nations are settled by appeals to force, and not to justice, the stronger nations soon demonstrate that they are right. While the majority of men have outgrown the notion that a pugilist is in the right and an invalid is in the wrong because the former can thrash the latter, an analogous opinion is still entertained by those nations that rely solely on arms to vindicate the right.

Wars have been profitable to the military class and some of the capitalist class. The military class obtain salaries, positions and honors; the capitalist class receive interest on war debts, and profits from making guns and battleships and furnishing supplies. But the great body of a nation does not profit by war. A nation that conquers another by invasion never receives an indemnity equal to the expense of the war, or the conquering nation would have no war debt; and the victorious nations have the largest war debts, while the conquered nations have the smallest war debts. The nations that have the largest armies and make the most conquests have less wealth per capita than the nations which have small armies or none at all. This proves that war is not profitable to nations, and it also proves that in going to war nations do not act from motives of "economic interests," as is claimed by those who try to explain all human phenomena by "economic interests." It is only a few who profit by war; "economic interests" do not control the majority, or there would have been no war.

One of the favorite arguments in this country in defense of war is that we owe to it the freeing of the slaves. But such is not the case. Thirty years before the war William Lloyd Garrison, Wendell Phillips, and a few co-workers, without money or followers, in 1830 started the abolition movement, which gathered force by years of work until, in 1860, about half the people of the United States were converted to their cause. When abolition was in the air, when it was very apparent that it was to be accomplished by the educational method, that happened which has always happened in great world movements: the military class rushed in and said, We will settle this question with the sword; we will convert the other half of the people, not by arguments, as was the first half, but by force; if any are killed they will not need to be converted. It is reasonable to infer that if the same process that had converted the first half of the nation had been permitted to continue, it would have converted the rest of the people or enough to assure the success of the abolition of slavery without war. The educational work of Garrison, Phillips and others did not cost the nation a dollar, but the war cost thousands of lives and incurred a war debt of millions of dollars, the interest on which our children's children will pay forever.[18]

How is war to be abolished? By going to war? Is bloodshed to be stopped by the shedding of blood? No; the way to stop war is to stop going to war; stop supporting it and it will fall, just as slavery did, just as the Inquisition did. The end of war is in sight; there will be no more world wars. The laboring-man, who has always done the fighting, is losing his patriotism; he is beginning to realize that he has no country or much of anything else to fight for, and is beginning to decline the honor of being killed for the glory and profits of the few. And those who profit by war, those who own the country, will not fight for it; that is, they are not patriotic if it is necessary for them to do the killing or to be killed in war. In all the wars of history there are very few instances of the rich meeting their death on the battlefield.

Soon there will be no poor so foolish as to go to war; not because it has become unprofitable, for it has never been profitable; but because social consciousness has been developed by the teachings of the great Libertarians, who have always stood for peace. Liberty leads to peace, while authority necessarily leads to war. Lovers of liberty are willing to compare the lives of those who stood for liberty with those who have stood for authority, of those who have tried to save with those who have tried to destroy.

---

[18] As of the writing of this footnote (December 2018), Irene Triplett, an 87-year old daughter of a Civil War soldier, was still receiving a monthly pension payment, 153 years after the war ended.

Industrial vs. Militant Type

Those who would rather fight than work are of the Militant type; those who would rather work than fight are of the Industrial type, and now outnumber the former more than a hundred to one. Savagery and barbarism developed the Militant type; civilization introduced the Industrial type. Herbert Spencer has traced the origin, development, functions and decline of the Militant type; he has described the origin, development and functions of the Industrial type, and the evidences of its ultimate supremacy. There was a time when most men were warriors; but as industry developed, fewer and fewer went to war, until only a small minority did so, and governments were forced to draft men to serve; and of late years governments have to instill ideas of war into the plastic minds of school children in order to keep alive the dying embers of militancy.[19] The United States government spends millions of dollars yearly in luring,—by means of advertisements in newspapers, on billboards and moving pictures,—young men to enlist in sufficient numbers to keep its standing army fully recruited.

The distinguishing characteristic of the militant class is parasitism: the power and ability to destroy, to wage war and levy tribute, to impose arbitrary restrictions and collect taxes, to take and to consume; in short, to govern.

For countless ages the industrial class has been oppressed and despoiled by the militant class, but now it is coming into its own, and holds the future of the race in its hands. The industrial class possesses one power that is distinctively and exclusively its own: it is an economic power: the industrial class produces all, builds all, exchanges all. The realization of its irresistible power and the knowledge of how to use it will bring its emancipation.

---

[19] An example from an American school textbook: "The Liberty Reader was made to meet the wide-felt need of a book compiled from the literature of the war, which would be suitable for boys and girls of elementary-school age. Teachers everywhere have been alive to the duty of the school to implant in the minds and hearts of their pupils a knowledge and an appreciation of the ideals that lie behind this great war for human liberty, and to make potent as an influence in their young lives the glorious examples of heroism and sacrifice and service which have already sanctified the struggle."—Bernard M. Sheridan, *The Liberty Reader* (Chicago: Benj. H Sanborn & Co., 1920).

When the workingman realizes that war does not benefit him, but robs him, the militant class will not be able to hire him or force him to go to war; and if the industrial class refuses to use its economic power for the benefit of the militant parasites, one of these classes must disappear—and it will not be the industrial! Only so long as the militant class can induce the industrial class to support it will it survive. When the worker learns that he belongs to the industrial class and not to the militant class, that his power is economic and not military, the economic problem will be solved.

The laboring-men who still prattle of revolution, meaning by that term warfare, and those labor "leaders" who imagine they can gain something for their cause by violence, are half a century behind the times. Can they not see that violence is the game of their oppressors? and do they hope to beat them at their own game? They might be able to throw a few dynamite bombs by hand, but the war-machines of the soldiers can throw them at the rate of twenty per second. The industrial class cannot compete with the military class in the art of war; if it could, it would cease to be industrial and become militant.

Individuals may do this, but the race has passed that period of its development. The man who thinks the industrial class can progress by any other then industrial methods does not understand economic forces; he is in the wrong class; he should join the army; he is betraying the laboring class when he advocates militant measures. In this country not one workingman in a hundred can handle a gun as well as a soldier can, and yet some labor leaders insist on war talk and the singing of war songs like the "Marseillaise" and "The Red Flag."

Flags

A flag is an emblem of warfare; when unfurled, it is a challenge to combat. Are the laboring-men able and willing to defend a war emblem on the battlefield? If so, then they are of the Militant type and not of the Industrial type. But the fact is they cannot successfully defend their flag in battle. They must cure themselves of this war disease, and learn to use their industrial power instead. The economic or industrial power is sufficient if intelligently used. It is industrial freedom that the laboring man needs, not military despotism, and industrial freedom must come from industrial action and not from military action.

The Mexican Revolution is an attempt by many of the dispossessed to regain the lands taken from them by their government and given or sold cheaply to big corporations. Their cause is just, but their method of war is the worst that could be chosen, for if it succeeds it will only convert an agricultural class into a military class, without any gain to the workingman. Just follow the history of these military movements. Porfirio Diaz by military power overthrew the ruler before him, and continued his reign by this power; then Francisco Madero overthrew Diaz by military power, and the laboring-man was as bad off as before; then Madero was overthrown by Felix Diaz by military power; and thus the game would go on forever if the deluded laboring-man would continue to furnish the wealth and lives necessary to play it.

On the other hand, a few wise laboring-men in Mexico have used the industrial or economic method, and if anything is gained in this revolution, it will be due to this small peaceable minority. They have taken possession of land, and refused to pay rent for it. This is the passive method, so effective in the hands of intelligent men. It is the opposite of the military method, which is active. The passive method is suitable to the Industrial type, but is fatal to the Militant type; the difference in method arises from the difference in type. The military class can take, but cannot give; it can consume, but it cannot produce; it can destroy, but it cannot build; it can kill, but it cannot create. The industrial class possesses the economic power to produce, to create, to build. The laboring-man must realize that his only power is industrial, and rely on it to win his cause.

War will cease, and this will be due to intellectual development and the acceptance of the principle of liberty, which leads to justice. The humane spirit is at last coming uppermost, and the men who have brought this about are the great educators of the race—the great Libertarians whose arguments constitute this book, and whose names will live as long as men love liberty.

Quotations

Force is no remedy.—*John Bright.*[1]

◊

Freedom is a new religion, the religion of our time.—*Heine.*[2]

◊

Force and fraud are in war the two cardinal virtues.—*Hobbes.*[3]

◊

It is difficult to free fools from the chains they revere.—*Voltaire.*[4]

◊

When the state is corrupt then the laws are most multiplied.—*Tacitus.*[5]

◊

Law grinds the poor, and the rich men rule the law.—*Oliver Goldsmith.*[6]

---

[1] John Bright (1811-1889), British radical liberal and free-trade advocate, founder of the Anti-Corn League. These lines are from a speech given to the Birmingham Junior Liberal Association in 1880.

[2] Heinrich Heine (1797-1856), German poet, friend of Marx. This line is from his *English Fragments* (1828).

[3] Thomas Hobbes (1588-1679), English political philosopher, author of *The Leviathan* (1651), from which this quotation came.

[4] Voltaire, *nom de plume* of François Marie Arouet (1694-1778), prolific French writer and wit, a stone in the sandal of authority, and an all-around lover of liberty.

[5] Publius Cornelius Tacitus (c. 56-120 A.D.), Roman senator and historian. The quotation here is from his *Annales*, a history that treated the Empire from Tiberius to Nero. In the original it was, "Corruptissima re publica plurimae leges."

[6] Oliver Goldsmith (1728-1774), Irish novelist and playwright. The quotation is from his acclaimed poem, "The Traveller" (1764).

The free man is as courageous in timely retreat as in combat.—*Spinoza.*[7]

◊

Desire nothing for yourself which you do not desire for others.—*Spinoza.*

◊

Liberty is rendered even more precious by the recollection of servitude.
    —*Cicero.*[8]

◊

I wish men to be free, as much from mobs as kings,—from you as me.
    —*Byron.*[9]

◊

Freedom degenerates unless it has to struggle in its own defence.
    —*Lord Acton.*[10]

◊

The liberty of the individual is a necessary postulate of human progress.
    —*Ernest Renan.*[11]

◊

We have all of us sufficient fortitude to bear the misfortunes of others.
    —*Rochefoucauld.*[12]

---

[7] Baruch Spinoza (1632-1677), Dutch/Portuguese/Jewish moral philosopher. This quotation (and the one following) is from his *Ethics, Demonstrated in Geometrical Order,* published posthumously in 1677.

[8] Marcus Tullius Cicero (106 B.C.-43 B.C), Roman consul, senator, lawyer, orator and stoic philosopher. Cicero was among those declared an enemy of the state by the Second Triumvirate and thereafter assassinated. The quotation, from his Third Philippic, was "Iucundiorem autem faciet libertatem servitutis recordatio."

[9] Lord Byron (1788-1824), one of the leading English romantic poets. The quotation is from his satiric poem, "Don Juan" (1824).

[10] John Dalberg-Acton, 1st Baron Acton (1834-1902), British historian, politician, a liberal in the old sense of the word. The quotation can be found in "Conflicts with Rome" in his *The History of Freedom and Other Essays.*

[11] Joseph Ernest Renan (1823-1892), French philosopher, biblical scholar. The quotation is from *The Future of Science* (1893) which, despite its title, is an examination of religious history in light of the author's experience in the Revolutions of 1848.

[12] François de La Rochefoucauld (1613-1680, French aristocrat, aphorist and memoirist. This quotation is from *Moral Reflections, Sentences and Maxims,* probably the 1851 English translation.

Men in earnest have no time to waste in patching fig leaves for the naked truth.—*Lowell.*[13]

◊

The concealment of truth is the only indecorum known to science. —*Edvard Westermarck.*[14]

◊

Liberty of thought is a mockery of liberty if speech and action is denied. —*Rev. Sidney Holmes.*[15]

◊

Liberty is not a means to a higher political end. It is itself the highest political end.—*Lord Acton.*[16]

◊

Where slavery is there liberty cannot be, and where liberty is there slavery cannot be.—*Charles Sumner.*[17]

◊

God grants liberty only to those who live it, and are always ready to guard and defend it.—*Daniel Webster.*[18]

---

[13] James Russell Lowell (1819-1891), American poet, editor and abolitionist. His poem, "A Glance Behind the Curtain," is the source of this quotation.

[14] Edvard Westermarck (1862-1939), Finnish sociologist and freethinker. His book, *The History of Human Marriage*, is the source of this quotation.

[15] I have found no mention of this author, or source for this quotation.

[16] From a speech, "The History of Freedom in Antiquity," given at the Bridgnorth Institute, 26 February 1877.

[17] Charles Sumner (1811-1874), U.S. Senator from Massachusetts, leader of the "Radical Republicans." A staunch abolitionist, Sumner was infamously beaten unconscious on the floor of the U.S. Senate by Preston Brooks, a congressman from South Carolina, in 1856. The quotation is from a speech, "Slavery and the Rebellion One and Indivisible."

[18] Daniel Webster (1782-1852), American lawyer and politician, famed for his eloquence. This quotation appears to have been miscopied. The original, from a 3 June 1834 speech in the U.S. Senate, was "God grants liberty only to those who **love** it..."

Man has a right to think all things, speak all things, write all things, but not to impose his opinions.—*Machiavelli.*[19]

◊

If you would achieve undying fame, attach yourself to the most unpopular righteous cause.—*George William Curtis.*[20]

◊

Society can overlook murder, adultery or swindling; it never forgives the preaching of a new gospel.—*Frederic Harrison.*[21]

◊

I don't believe in capital punishment, Hinnissy, but 'twill never be abolished while th' people injie it so much.—*Mr. Dooley.*[22]

◊

There is one thing in the world more wicked than the desire to command, and that is the will to obey.—*William Kingdon Clifford.*[23]

◊

All our liberties are due to men who, when their conscience has compelled them, have broken the laws of the land.—*Dr. Clifford.*[24]

---

[19] Niccolò Machiavelli (1469-1527), Italian Renaissance politician and writer, author of the political treatise, *The Prince.* This quotation, although attributed to Machiavelli in several political tracts in the late 19th and early 20th century, was never accompanied by a reference to a specific work of his. I am skeptical of this attribution.

[20] George William Curtis (1824-1892), American writer, supporter of the nascent Republican Party. No source or confirmation of this quotation was located.

[21] Frederic Harrison (1831-1923), English jurist and radical. This line is from his essay on John Ruskin, "Unto This Last." (Not to be confused with Ruskin's essay of the same title.)

[22] Mr. Dooley was a fictional Irish bartender created by American journalist Finley Peter Dunne (1867-1936). In a popular newspaper column of the day, Mr. Dooley debated public affairs with a bar patron, Malachi Hennessy. I find it helps to affect an Irish accent, at least in my imagination, when reading this.

[23] William Kingdon Clifford (1845-1879), English mathematician, of "Clifford algebra" fame. This quotation is attributed to Clifford in the introduction, by Frederick Pollock, of the 1901 *Lectures and Essays by the Late William Kingdon Clifford, F.R.S.,* though this line is not cited, nor does it appear within the items of this collection.

[24] John Clifford (1836-1923), English non-conformist minister, early advocate of passive resistance. The source of the quotation has not been identified.

They that can give up essential liberty to obtain a little temporary safety deserve neither liberty nor safety.—*Benjamin Franklin.*[25]

◊

It will be found an unjust and unwise jealousy to deprive a man of his natural liberty upon a supposition he may abuse it.—*Cromwell.*[26]

◊

It is doubtful whether any tyranny can be worse than that exercised in the name of the sovereignty of the people.—*George L. Scherger.*[27]

◊

It is not the disease, but the physician; it is the pernicious hand of government alone which can reduce a whole people to despair.—*Junius.*[28]

◊

Rayformers, Hinnissy, is in favor iv suppressin' iverything, but rale pollyticians believes in suppressin' nawthin' but ividence.—*Mr. Dooley.*

◊

Every citizen may freely speak, write or print on any subject, being responsible for the abuse of that liberty.—*Constitution of Pennsylvania.*[29]

---

[25] Benjamin Franklin (1706-1790), American philosopher, publisher, scientist, diplomat, politician, inventor. This famous line was in a 1775 letter from Franklin, urging the colonists to stay firm in their demands during their last-ditch attempt to achieve reconciliation with Parliament.

[26] Oliver Cromwell (1599-1658), Puritan, regicide, Lord Protector of England. This line is from a 12 September 1650 letter from Cromwell to the Governor of Edinburgh Castle.

[27] George L. Scherger (1874-1941), American pastor, musician and historian. This line is from his 1904 book, *The Evolution of Modern Liberty.*

[28] "Junius pseudonym of an author who wrote political letters critical of King George III, printed in London's *Public Advertiser* newspaper from 1769 to 1772. A volume, *The Letters of Junius: Stat Nominis Umbra,* was published in 1813, giving a date of 21 January 1769 for the quotation given above.

[29] Article 7 differs by one word from the above: "The free communication of thoughts and opinions is one of the invaluable rights of man, and every citizen may freely speak, write **and** print on any subject, being responsible for the abuse of that liberty."

Liberty which is the nurse of all great wits…. Give me the liberty to know, to utter, and to argue freely according to conscience, above all liberties.—*Milton.*[30]

◊

An ambassador is a man who goes abroad to lie for the good of his country. A journalist is a man who stays at home to pursue the same vocation. —*Dr. S. Johnson.*[31]

◊

To argue against any breach of liberty from the ill use that may be made of it, is to argue against liberty itself, since all is capable of being abused. —*Lord Lyttleton.*[32]

◊

I'll niver go down again to see sojers off to th' war. But ye'll see me at th' depot with a brass band whin th' men that causes wars starts f'r th' scene iv carnage.—*Mr. Dooley.*

◊

Did the mass of men know the actual selfishness and injustice of their rulers, not a government would stand a year; the world would ferment with Revolution.—*Theodore Parker.*[33]

---

[30] John Milton (1608-1674), epic English poet of the English epic poem, *Paradise Lost.* This quotation is from *Areopagitica* (1644), his defense of free speech.

[31] Samuel Johnson a.k.a. Dr. Johnson (1709-1784), eminent English man of letters, lexicographer, journalist, poet, wit, and subject of a famous biography, Boswell's *Life of Samuel Johnson.* Unfortunately, I do not find this line in Johnson. Although the start of the line has a precedent in Sir Henry Wotton in 1603 ("An ambassador is an honest gentleman sent to lie abroad for the good of his country"), the first located occurrence of the cynical conclusion was in the 27 October 1913 *Baltimore Sun*, in H.L Mencken's column, "The Free Lance." Although it is there attributed to Dr. Johnson, I suspect, by the tone of it, that this was a Mencken creation, and an ironic, self-referential one at that.

[32] George Lyttelton, 1st Baron Lyttelton (1709-1373), a minor British statesman and an even more minor English poet. His 1735 *Letters from a Persian in England, to his Friend at Ispahan*, letter XLVIII, is the source of the above quotation.

[33] Theodore Parker (1810-1860), American transcendentalist, Unitarian minister and abolitionist. The quotation is from a sermon, "Of Justice and the Conscience," number five of those published in his *Ten Sermons of Religion and Prayer.*

It takes great strength to live where you belong
When other people think that you are wrong.
—*Charlotte Perkins Gilman.*[34]

◊

All of our greatness was born of liberty, even our commercialism was rocked in the cradle of democracy, and we cannot strangle the mother without destroying her children.—*Altgeld.*[35]

◊

We crave for the good opinion of the world, in which we don't believe, and tremble in face of its condemnation, which we despise and condemn in our hearts.—*Hermann Sudermann.*[36]

◊

A temporal government in the hands of ecclesiastics develops into a mild, petty, listless, respectable, monkish, invincible despotism just as any plant develops into its flower.—*Taine.*[37]

◊

Is life so dear, or peace so sweet, as to be purchased at the price of chains and slavery? I know not what course others may take, but as for me, give me liberty or give me death!—*Patrick Henry.*[38]

---

[34] Charlotte Perkins Gilman (1860-1935), American poet, social reformer and utopian feminist. The above lines are from her poem, "Heroism," from *In This Our World* (1895).

[35] John Peter Altgeld (1847-1902), German-born American politician, Governor of Illinois, leading Progressive Democrat. A speech at the University of Michigan, 14 December 1901, is the source of this quotation.

[36] Hermann Sudermann (1857-1928), German dramatist. The above quotation is from the 1898 English translation, by Beatrice Marshall, of Sudermann's play, *Regina or The Sins of the Fathers.*

[37] Hippolyte Taine (1828-1893), French historian and literary critic. The quotation is slightly abridged from the original, which appeared in Taine's published travel journal, *Italy: Rome and Naples.*

[38] Patrick Henry (1736-1799), Virginian, American Founding Father. The quotation, from Patrick's famous speech to the Second Virginia Convention assembled at Richmond, March 23, 1775, omits the exclamation, "Forbid it, Almighty God!" which came between these two lines.

All truth is safe, and nothing else is safe; and he who keeps back the truth or withholds it from men, from motives of expediency, is either a coward, or a criminal, or both.—*Max Muller*.[39]

◊

Everywhere the strong have made the laws and oppressed the weak; and, if they have sometimes consulted the interests of society, they have always forgotten those of humanity.—*Turgot*.[40]

◊

The persecuting spirit has its origin morally in the disposition of man to domineer over his fellow creatures; intellectually, in the assumption that one's own opinions are infallibly correct.—*John Fiske*.[41]

◊

The freest government cannot long endure when the tendency of the law is to create a rapid accumulation of property in the hands of a few, and to render the masses poor and dependent.—*Daniel Webster*.[42]

◊

The fancy that war is necessary to maintain the ideals of manly courage is as mistaken as is the notion that the system of the duel was required to uphold the sense of personal honor.—*Nathaniel Southgate Shaler*.[43]

---

[39] Friedrich Max Müller (1823-1900), German scholar of comparative religion. Although several anarchist publications gave his *Science of Religion* as the source of this quotation, an examination of the 1870, 1872 and 1893 editions of that work could not locate this line.

[40] Doubtful. No occurrence found before an 1880 anthology of *A Thousand Flashes of French Wit, Wisdom and Wickedness*, a hundred years after Turgot's death.

[41] John Fiske (1842-1901), American philosopher, proponent of seemingly incompatible views, being both an abolitionist and being a proponent of "scientific" racism. His paper, "The Philosophy of Persecution" (*North American Review*, January, 1881), is the source of the above quotation.

[42] Doubtful. I've found no use of this phrase before it became popular with early 20th century labor activists. (Webster died in 1852.)

[43] Nathaniel Southgate Shaler (1841-1906), American geologist who also speculated and wrote on religion and evolution. *The Individual: A Study of Life and Death* (1900) is the source of the above quotation.

Every citizen may freely speak, write and publish his sentiments on all subjects, being responsible for the abuse of that liberty. No law shall ever be passed to curtail or restrain the liberty of speech or of the press. —*Constitution of Connecticut.*

◊

The good of mankind is a dream if it is not to be secured by preserving for all men the possible maximum of liberty of action and of freedom of thought. —*John M. Robertson.*[44]

◊

For always in thine eyes, O Liberty!
Shines that high light whereby the world is saved;
And, though thou slay us, we will trust in thee.
—*John Hay.*[45]

◊

'Tis a good thing preachers don't go to Congress. Whin they're ca'm they'd wipe out all th' laws, an' whin they're excited, they'd wipe out all th' popylation. They're niver two jumps fr'm th' thumbcrew.—Mr. Dooley.

◊

To this thought I cling, with virtue rife,
Wisdom's last fruit profoundly true.
Freedom alone he earns as well as life,
Who day by day must conquer them anew.
—*Goethe.*[46]

---

[44] John Mackinnon Robertson (1856-1933), British journalist and politician. Among his early works was the book, *Modern Humanists* (1901), in which the above quotation can be found.

[45] John Hay (1838-1905), Secretary of State under William McKinley and Theodore Roosevelt, author of an early Lincoln biography (Hay was Lincoln's private secretary), and a minor poet. The final lines of his early poem, "Liberty," provide our quotation.

[46] Johann Wolfgang von Goethe (1749-1832), preeminent German literary figure. His *magnum opus* was his verse drama, *Faust*, in Part II of which the titular character speaks the above lines.

Everyone may seek his own happiness in the way that seems good to himself, provided that he infringe not such freedom of others to strive after a similar end as is consistent with the freedom of all according to a possible general law.—*Kant*.[47]

◊

Although I am not such a fanatic for the liberty of the subject as to plead that interfering with the way in which a man may choose to be killed is a violation of that liberty, yet I do think that it is far better to let everybody do as he likes.—*Huxley*.[48]

◊

To mind your own business and do the square thing with your neighbors is an extremely high order of patriotism. If every man were to do this, flags, governments, powers, dominations and thrones might all take an indefinite vacation.—*Puck*.[49]

◊

And this is Liberty—that one grow after the law of his own life, hindering not another; and this is Opportunity; and the fruit thereof is Variation; and from the glad growing and the fruit-feasting comes Sympathy, which is appreciative and helpful good-fellowship.—*J. Wm. Lloyd*.[50]

◊

He's true to God who's true to man; where ever wrong is done,
To the humblest and the weakest, 'neath the all-beholding sun,
That wrong is also done to us, and they are slaves most base,
Whose love of right is for themselves and not for all the race.
    —*[James Russell] Lowell*.[51]

---

[47] Immanuel Kant (1724-1804), German arch-philosopher. The above quotation is from his essay, "The Natural Principle of the Political Order," published in translation in 1891 as Kant's *Principles of Politics* (Edinburgh: Clark, 1891).

[48] Thomas Henry Huxley (1825-1895), English biologist and advocate for the theory of evolution (he was called "Darwin's bulldog"). This quotation is from his 1884 essay, "The State and the Medical Profession."

49 *Puck* (1871-1918), American humor magazine, often featuring political satire. No specific source of this quotation has been identified.

[50] John William Lloyd (1857-1940), American individualist anarchist, publisher of an anarchist magazine, *The Free Comrade*, the prospectus for which contained the above quotation.

[51] From his poem, "On the Capture of Fugitive Slaves Near Washington." This passage was a favorite of the American socialists and appeared frequently in their publications. Eugene V. Debs drew on these remarks in a statement during his 1918 sedition trial.

Let us all seek truth as if none of us had possession of it. The opinions which to this day have governed the earth, produced by chance, disseminated in obscurity, admitted without discussion, credited from a love of novelty and imitation, have in a manner clandestinely usurped their empire.—*Volney.*[52]

◊

There is tonic in the things that men do not love to hear; and there is damnation in the things that wicked men love to hear. Free speech is to a great people what winds are to oceans and malarial regions, which waft away the elements of disease, and bring new elements of health; and where free speech is stopped miasma is bred, and death comes fast.—*Henry Ward Beecher.*[53]

◊

In Russia, whenever they catch a man, woman, or child that has got any brains or education or character, they ship that person straight to Siberia. It is admirable, it is wonderful. It is so searching and so effective that it keeps the general level of Russian intellect and education down to that of the czar. —*Mark Twain.*[54]

◊

The great truth has finally gone forth to all the ends of the earth that man shall no more render account to man for his belief, over which he has himself no control. Henceforward nothing shall prevail upon us to praise or to blame any one for that which he can no more change than he can the hue of his skin or the height of his stature.—*Lord Brougham.*[55]

---

[52] Constantin François de Chassebœuf, comte de Volney (1757-1820), French philosopher and historian. His 1796 *The Ruins: A Survey of the Revolutions of Empires* is the source of this quotation.

[53] Henry Ward Beecher (1813-1887), American minister and abolitionist, brother of Harriet Beecher Stowe of *Uncle Tom's Cabin* fame. The quotation is from a sermon, "Peace, Be Still," preached at Plymouth Church, Brooklyn, New York, 4 January 1861.

[54] Mark Twain, the pen name of Samuel Langhorne Clemens (1935-1910), American journalist, novelist and humorist. The quotation is from his novel, *The American Claimant* (1892)

[55] Henry Peter Brougham, 1st Baron Brougham and Vaux (1778-1868), British statesman, liberal, Lord Chancellor (1830-1834). The quotation is from a 6 April 1825 address at the University of Glasgow on his installation as Lord Rector.

In those days there was no king in Israel, but every man did that which was right in his own eyes.

And as ye would that men should do to you, do ye also to them likewise. If the truth shall make you free, ye shall be freed indeed. He that knoweth to do good and doeth it not, to him it is sin.—*Bible.*[56]

◊

The constitution of man is such that for a long time after he has discovered the incorrectness of the ideas prevailing around him, he shrinks from openly emancipating himself from their domination; and constrained by the force of circumstances, he becomes a hypocrite, publicly applauding what his private judgment condemns. —*Dr. J. W. Draper.*[57]

◊

The whole progress of society consists in learning how to attain, by the independent action or voluntary association of individuals, those objects which are at first attempted only through the agency of government, and in lessening the sphere of legislation and enlarging that of the individual reason and conscience. —*Samuel J. Tilden.*[58]

◊

> Open thine eyes to see,
> Slave, and thy feet are free.
> Thy bonds, and thy beliefs are one in kind,
> And of thy fears thine irons wrought.
> Hang weights about thee fashioned out of thine own thought.
> —*Swinburne.*[59]

---

[56] A mashup of three different verses: Luke 6:31, John 8:36, James 4:17, where the passage from John is mangled. It should be "If the Son therefore shall make you free, ye shall be free indeed."

[57] John William Draper (1811-1882), American chemist, pioneering photographer and historian. The quotation is from his *History of the Intellectual Development of Europe,* Volume 1 (1864). Note: the original has, "...he **lives** a hypocrite..."

[58] Samuel Jones Tilden (1814-1886), American politician, presidential candidate who won a majority of the popular vote in 1876, and would have won the Electoral College, but lost to Rutherford B. Hayes in a backroom deal that allowed the Republican to win in return for withdrawing troops from the South, ending Reconstruction. This remarkable line is from a 3 October 1855 letter expressing a negative opinion on "coercive temperance."

[59] Algernon Charles Swiburne (1837-1909), English poet and playwright. The quotation is from his poem, "The Eve of Revolution."

Of what use is freedom of thought, if it will not produce freedom of action, which is the sole end, how remote soever in appearance, of all objections against Christianity? And therefore the free thinkers consider it an edifice where all the parts have such a mutual dependence on each other, that, if you pull out one single nail, the whole fabric must fall to the ground.—*Swift.*[60]

◊

The modern reformist, Philosophy, which annihilates the individual by way of aiding the mass, and the late reformist, Legislation, which prohibits pleasure with the view of advancing happiness, seem to be chips of that old block of a French feudal law which, to prevent young partridges from being disturbed, imposed penalties upon hoeing and weeding.—*Edgar Allen Poe.*[61]

◊

The law of nature, being co-eval with mankind, and dictated by God himself, is superior in obligation to every other. It is binding all over the globe, in all countries, and at all times; no human laws are of any validity if contrary to this, and such of them as are valid derive their force and all their authority, mediately or immediately, from the original.—*Blackstone.*[62]

◊

O sorrowing hearts of slaves,
We heard you beat from far!
We bring the light that saves,
We bring the morning star;
Freedom's good things we bring you,
Whence all good things are.
—*Algernon Charles Swinburne.*[63]

---

[60] Jonathan Swift (1667-1745), an Anglo-Irish satirist, from his 1708 essay, "An Argument to Prove that the Abolishing of Christianity in England May, As Things Now Stand, Be Attended With Some Inconveniences, and Perhaps Not Produce Those Many Good Effects Proposed Thereby." The essay was satirical, though it appears that Sprading did not see that, in context, the lines quoted were ironic.

[61] Edgar Allen Poe (1809-1849), American author and poet. The quotation is No. 262 of his "Marginalia," originally attached to his copy of the July, 1849 issue of *Southern Literary Messenger*.

[62] Sir William Blackstone (1723-1780), English jurist, author of *Commentaries on the Law of England* (four volumes, published 1765-69), a treatise on the common law, influential in England and in America. The introduction to section two, "Of the Nature of Laws in General," is the source of the quotation.

63 From "A Marching Song."

In the twentieth century war will be dead, the scaffold will be dead, royalty will be dead, and dogmas will be dead; but man will live. For all, there will be but one country—that country the whole earth; for all, there will be but one hope—that hope the whole heaven. All hail, then, to that noble twentieth century, which shall own our children, and which our children shall inherit.—*Victor Hugo.*[64]

◊

Over against Nature stands the Man, and deep in his heart is the passion for liberty. For the passion for liberty is only another name for life itself. Liberty is a word of much sophistication, but it means, when it means anything, opportunity to live one's own life in one's own way. . . . The original sin of the world is not contempt for arbitrary laws, but respect for them. . . . —*Rev. Charles Ferguson.*[65]

◊

Without free speech no search for truth is possible; without free speech no discovery of truth is useful; without free speech progress is checked and the nations no longer march forward toward the nobler life which the future holds for man. Better a thousand fold abuse of free speech than denial of free speech. The abuse dies in a day, but the denial slays the life of the people and entombs the hope of the race.—*Charles Bradlaugh.*[66]

◊

Bigotry has no head and cannot think, no heart and cannot feel. When she moves it is in wrath; when she pauses it is amid ruin. Her prayers are curses, her God is a demon, her communion is death, her vengeance is eternity, her

---

[64] Victor Hugo (1802-1885), French novelist, poet and exile, from his "Address to the Workman's Congress at Marseille" (1879).

[65] Charles Ferguson (1863-?), American layer, minister and author. The quotation is from his *The Affirmative Intellect: An Account of the Origin and Mission of the American Spirit* (1901).

[66] Charles Bradlaugh (1833-1891), English politician and atheist. Elected Member of Parliament, he was fined, imprisoned, and removed from office for his refusal to take a religious oath to be seated in the House of Commons. He was reelected by his constituents, and eventually permitted to make a "solemn affirmation" instead of an oath. Although these lines have been frequently repeated, I have found no source in Bradlaugh's works.

decalogue written in the blood of her victims, and if she stops for a moment in her infernal flight it is upon a kindred rock to whet her vulture fang for a more sanguinary desolation.—*Daniel O'Connell.*[67]

◊

The man of virtuous soul commands not, nor obeys.

Power, like a desolating pestilence,

Pollutes whate'er it touches;

.... and obedience,

Bane of all genius, virtue, freedom, truth,

Makes slaves of men, and, of the human frame,

A mechanized automaton.

—*Shelley.*[68]

◊

Self-love is a necessary, indestructible, universal law and principle, insepa-rable from every kind of love. Religion must and does confirm this on every page of her history. Wherever man tries to resist that human egoism, whether in religion, philosophy, or politics, he sinks into pure nonsense and insanity; for the sense which forms the egoism of all human instincts, desires and actions, is the satisfaction of the human being, the satisfaction of human egoism.—*Feuerbach.*[69]

---

[67] Daniel O'Connell (1775-1847), Irish politician, proponent of Catholic emancipa-tion. Although these lines are widely attributed to O'Connell, I have found no citation of a specific publication, letter or speech. The earliest instance of these words that I have found was the 1819, *A Word of Advice to the Reformers in General, and to Those of Birmingham in Particular*, by the pseudonymous, "Philanthropos."

[68] Percy Bysshe Shelley (1792-1822), English poet and radical. His utopian poem, "Queen Mab," is the source of the quotation.

[69] Ludwig Feuerbach (1804-1872), German philosopher. These lines are slightly abridged from the version quoted in "The Perception of the Infinite," in F. Max Mueller, *Lectures on the Origin and Growth of Religion* (1880), p. 20, where it is attributed to Feurbach's *Das Wesen der Religion*, p.100.

I say discuss all and expose all—I am for every topic openly;
I say there can be no safety for these States without innovators—
     without free tongues, and ears willing to hear the tongues;
And I announce as a glory of these States, that they respectfully
     listen to propositions, reforms, fresh views and doctrines,
     from successions of men and women.
Each age with its own growth!
—*Walt Whitman.*[70]

◊

Of all the miserable, unprofitable, inglorious wars in the world is the war against words. Let men say just what they like. Let them propose to cut every throat and burn every house—if so they like it. We have nothing to do with a man's words or a man's thoughts, except to put against them better words and better thoughts, and so to win in the great moral and intellectual duel that is always going on, and on which all progress depends.—*Auberon Herbert.*[71]

◊

And this freedom will be the freedom of all. It will loosen both master and slave from the chain. For, by a divine paradox, wherever there is one slave there are two. So in the wonderful reciprocities of being, we can never reach the higher levels until all our fellows ascend with us. There is no true liberty for the individual except as he finds it in the liberty of all. There is no true security for the individual except as he finds it in the security of all. —*Edwin Markham.*[72]

---

[70] Walt Whitman (1819-1892), American poet and journalist. These lines are a slight variant of his poem "Says" from *Leaves of Grass*. The original has, "I say there can be no **salvation** for these States…"

[71] Auberon Edward William Molyneux Herbert (1838-1906), British politician, early proponent of voluntaryism. The quotation is widely ascribed to a 22 November 1893 letter to the *Westminster Gazette*.

[72] Edwin Markham (1852-1940), American poet. The quotation is from the "Notes" to his *The Man with a Hoe* (1900).

It is the greatest of all inconsistencies to wish to be other than we are.

The more a man has in himself, the less he will want from other people—the less, indeed, other people can be to him. This is why a high degree of intellect tends to make a man unsocial.

A man can be himself only so long as he is alone; and, if he does not love solitude, he will not love freedom; for it is only when he is alone that he is really free.—*Schopenhauer.*[73]

◊

Would to God that this hot and bloody struggle was over, and that peace may come at last to the world! And yet I invoke no seeming peace that the weaker may ever anon be plundered, but a peace with liberty, equality, and honest man's and not robber's order for its condition. . . . Let others give aid and comfort to despots. Be it ours to stand for liberty and justice, nor fear to lock arms with those who are called hot-heads and demagogues, when the good cause requires.—*Chas. A. Dana.*[74]

◊

They are slaves who fear to speak
For the fallen and the weak;
They are slaves who will not choose
Hatred, scoffing, and abuse
Rather than in silence shrink
From the truth they needs must think;
They are slaves who dare not be
In the right with two or three.
—*Lowell.*[75]

---

[73] Arthur Schopenhauer (1788-1860), German philosopher. The passage given is a literary sausage, ground up bits of several works, squeezed together including, "The Art of Controversy," *The Wisdom of Life*, and *Counsels and Maxims.*

[74] Charles Anderson Dana (1819-1897), American journalist. These lines are attributed to a letter on "The European Revolution" in *The Spirit of the Age*, 18 August 1849. (Probably a copy of his work for the *New York Tribune*.)

[75] From his poem, "Stanzas on Freedom."

If governments are to accept the principle that the only limits to the enforcement of the moral standard of the majority are the narrow expediencies of
each special case, without reference to any deep and comprehensive principle covering all the largest considerations, why, then, the society to which
we ought to look with most admiration and envy is the Eastern Empire
during the ninth and tenth centuries, when the Byzantine system of a thor-
ough subordination of the spiritual power had fully consolidated itself.
—*John Morley.*[76]

Power usurped

Is weakness when opposed; conscious of wrong
'Tis pusillanimous and prone to flight.
But slaves that once conceive the glowing thought
Of freedom, in that hope itself possess
All that the contest calls for—spirit, strength.
The scorn of danger and united hearts,
The surest presage of the good they seek.
—*Cowper.*[77]

◊

There was once a discussion between Mr. Pitt and some of his friends on
what were the qualities most needed in politics. Was it knowledge, patience,
courage, eloquence, or what was it? Mr. Pitt said, "Patience." We liberals have
tried patience for twenty years. I vote we now try "courage." I say again, don't
let us be afraid of our own shadows. We have principles we believe in, we have
faith, we have great traditions, and we have a great cause behind us and before
us. Let us not lose courage and straightforwardness.—*John Morley.*[78]

---

[76] John Morley (1838-1923), English liberal politician. The quotation is from his 1898
On Compromise, the concluding lines of his lengthy "Note to Page 242" (19 pages long),
where he presents, "a short exposition on liberty."
[77] William Cowper (1731-1800), English poet and abolitionist. These lines are from his
poem, "The Task" (1785).
[78] Often ascribed to Morley, but no source has been identified.

What greater life, what grander claim,
Than that which bids you to be just?
What brighter halo, fairer fame,
Than shines above the sacred dust
Of him who, formed of finer clay,
Stood firm, a hero of revolt
Against the weakness of his day,
The traitor's trick, the pander's fault?
—*Gordak*.[79]

◊

The enlargement of freedom has always been due to heretics who have been unrequited during their day and defamed when dead. No (other) publisher in any country ever incurred so much peril to free the press as Richard Carlile. Every British bookseller has profited by his intrepidity and endurance. Speculations of philosophy and science, which are now part of the common intelligence, power and profit, would have been stifled to this day but for him.—*George Jacob Holyoake*.[80]

◊

Fear not the tyrants shall rule forever,
Or the priests of the evil faith;
They stand on the brink of that mighty river
Whose waves they have tainted with death;
It is fed from the depths of a thousand dells,
Around them it foams and rages and swells,
And their swords and their scepters I floating see,
Like wrecks on the surge of eternity.
—*Shelley*.[81]

---

[79] William Walstein Gordak (1846-1903), American poet. A book of his poetry, *Here's Luck to Lora: And Other Poems*, was published posthumously, in 1906, by the famous individualist anarchist Benjamin R. Tucker. This puts Gordak in the libertarian sphere. The above quotation, however, does not occur in this volume, nor has any other source been identified.

[80] George Jacob Holyoake (1817-1906), English journalist, activist, proponent of secularism. These lines come from his 1892 autobiography, *Sixty Years of an Agitator's Life*.

[81] From his 1818 verse play, *Rosalind and Helen*.

The idea of governing by force another man, who I believe to be my equal in the sight of God, is repugnant to me. I do not want to do it. I do not want any one to govern me by any kind of force. I am a reasoning being, and I only need to be shown what is best for me, when I will take that course or do that thing simply because it is best, and so will you. I do not believe that a soul was ever forced toward anything except toward ruin.

Liberty for the few is not liberty. Liberty for me and slavery for you means slavery for both.—*Samuel M. Jones*.[82]

◊

Wherever bibliolatry has prevailed, bigotry and cruelty have accompanied it. It lies at the root of the deep-seated, sometimes disguised, but never absent, antago-nism of all the varieties of ecclesiasticism to the freedom of thought and to the spirit of scientific investigation. To those who look upon ignorance as one of the chief sources of evil, and hold veracity, not merely in act, but in thought, to be the one condition of true progress, whether moral or intellectual, it is clear that the biblical idol must go the way of all other idols, of infallibility in all shapes, lay or clerical.—*Thomas Henry Huxley*.[83]

◊

> Yet let us ponder boldly—'tis a base
> Abandonment of reason to resign
> Our right of thought—our last and only place
> Of refuge; this, at least, shall still be mine:
> Though from our birth the faculty divine
> Is chain'd and tortured—cabin'd, cribb'd, confined,
> And bred in darkness, lest the truth should shine
> Too brightly on the unprepared mind,
> The beam pours in, for time and skill will couch the blind.
> —*Byron*.[84]

---

[82] Samuel Milton "Golden Rule" Jones (1846-1904), Welsh-born, American manufac-turer and progressive-era politician. The first paragraph is quoted and ascribed to him in a 1906 biography by Ernest Crosby, *Golden Rule Jones: Mayor of Toledo*. No source for the last paragraph has been located.

[83] From the "Preface" to his *Science and Hebrew Tradition*.

[84] From his narrative poem, *Childe Harold's Pilgrimage*.

Do nothing to others which you would not have them do to you. Now I cannot see how, on this principle, one man is authorized to say to another, Believe what I believe, and what you cannot, or you shall be put to death. And yet this is said in direct terms in Portugal, Spain, and at Goa. In some other countries, indeed, they now content themselves with saying only, Believe as I do, or I shall hate you, and will do you all the mischief in my power. What an impious monster thou art! Not to be of my religion is to be of none. You ought to be held in abhorrence by your neighbors, your countrymen, and by all mankind.—*Voltaire*.[85]

◊

No revolution ever rises above the intellectual level of those who make it, and little is gained where one false notion supplants another. But we must some day, at last and forever, cross the line between nonsense and common sense. And on that day we shall pass from class paternalism, originally derived from the fetish fiction in times of universal ignorance, to human brotherhood in accordance with the nature of things and our growing knowledge of it; from political government to industrial administration; from competition in individualism to individuality in co-operation; from war and despotism in any form to peace and liberty.—*Carlyle*.[86]

◊

The State makes use of the money which it extorts from me to unjustly impose fresh constraints upon me; this is the case when it prescribes for me its theology or its philosophy, when it prescribes for me or denies me a special form of religious observance, when it pretends to regulate my morals and my manners, to limit my labor or my expenditure, to fix the price of my merchandise or the rate of my wages. With the coin which I do not owe it and which it steals from me it defrays the expense of the persecution which it inflicts upon me. Let us beware of the encroachments of the State, and suffer it to be nothing more than a watch-dog.—*Taine*.[87]

---

[85] From *A Treatise on Tolerance* (1763).

[86] Thomas Caryle (1795-1881), Scottish author and historian. The quotation is dubious, not found in any sources prior to occurring in early 20th century labor union newspapers.

[87] Appears to be based on Taine's essay, "Socialism as Government."

Now for the promised test, by which, when applied to a man, it may be seen whether the government he means to give his support to is of the one sort or of the other. Put him to this question: Will you, sir, or will you not, concur in putting matters on such a footing, in respect to the liberty of the press, and the liberty of public discussion, that, at the hands of the persons exercising the powers of government, a man shall have no more fear from speaking and writing against them, than from speaking and writing for them? If his answer be yes, the government he declares in favor of, is an undespotic one; if his answer be no, the government he declares in favor of, is a despotic one. —*Jeremy Bentham.*[88]

◊

Ideas are always liveliest when attempts are made to suppress them. The very worst way to suppress an idea is to attempt to suppress it. For, if an idea is true, you can't suppress it, and if it is false it does not need to be suppressed—it will suppress itself. If we all agreed finally and for good, talking would be nonsense. But because we disagree talking is the part of wisdom. The wise men who made the Constitution of the State of Pennsylvania knew this. So they advocated free speech. The men who today in Philadelphia make the administration of the laws foolish don't know it. So they advocate a despotism.—*Horace Traubel.*[89]

◊

Liberty of thought and speech have, after a prolonged struggle, been conceded, although there may be found people who, on their own pet failings, even yet refuse to allow the right unreservedly. Liberty of speech is justified on three grounds: First, if the opinion be true, the world reaps a benefit to be derived from the truth; secondly, if the opinion be false, truth is the more strengthened by contest with it, and lastly, if it be partly true and partly false, our opinions, if they do not entirely lose their weakness, at any rate gain the corrections which have greatly improved them. The commencement of the struggle was due to religion,

---

[88] Jeremy Bentham (1748-1832), English philosopher, father of utilitarianism. These lines are from his book. *On the Liberty of the Press and Public Discussion* (1821).
[89] Horace Traubel (1858-1919), American writer and socialist. His literary magazine, *The Conservator*, is the source of the above lines, from an essay, "Free Speech in Philadelphia or anywhere," published in the August 1909 issue.

and the man who brought the long fight to a close and finally settled that matter was Charles Bradlaugh.—*J. P. Poole.*[90]

There are no specious pretexts with which hypocrisy and tyranny have not colored their desire of imposing silence on men of discernment; and there is no virtuous citizen that can see in the pretexts any legitimate reason for their remaining silent. . . .

To limit the press is to insult the nation; to prohibit the reading of certain books is to declare the inhabitants to be either fools or slaves.

Should we to destroy error compel it to silence? No. How then? Let it talk on. Error, obscure of itself, is rejected by every sound understanding. If time have not given it credit, and it be not favored by government, it cannot bear the eye of examination. Reason will ultimately direct wherever it be freely exercised.—*Helvetius.*[91]

◊

I care not for the truth or error of the opinions held or uttered, nor for the wisdom of the words or time of their attempted expression, when I consider this great question of fundamental significance, this great fight which must first be secure before free society can be said to stand on any foundation, but only on temporary or capricious props.

Rich or poor, white or black, great or small, wise or foolish, in season or out of season, in the right or in the wrong, whosoever will speak, let him speak, and whosoever will hear, let him hear. And let no one pretend to the prerogative of judging another man's liberty. In this respect there is, and there can be, no superiority of persons or privileges, nor the slightest pretext for any. —*J. A. Andrews, Governor of Massachusetts.*[92]

---

[90] J. Parrington Poole (?-?), from an essay, "A Plea for the Liberty of the Individual," in the June 1898 issue of *The Westminster Review.*

[91] Claude Adrien Helvétius (1715-1771), a French *philosophe.* The quotation comes from his posthumous, *A Treatise on Man: His Intellectual Faculties and His Education.*

[92] John Albion Andrews (1818-1867), American politician and abolitionist. The quote is characterized as a letter written when Andrews was governor-elect, i.e., in 1860, according to Wendell Philips, in *Speeches, Lectures and Letters* (1894).

We will speak out, we will be heard,

Though all earth's systems crack;

We will not bate a single word,

Nor take a letter back.

[...]

Let liars fear, let cowards shrink,

Let traitors turn away;

Whatever we have dared to think

That dare we also say.

[...]

We speak the truth, and what care we

For hissing and for scorn,

While some faint gleamings we can see

Of Freedom's coming morn.

—*James R. Lowell.*[93]

◊

It is apprehended that arbitrary power would steal in upon us, were we not careful to prevent its progress, and were there not an easy method of conveying the alarm from one end of the kingdom to another. The spirit of the people must frequently be roused, in order to curb the ambition of the court, and the dread of rousing this spirit must be employed to prevent that ambition. Nothing is so effectual to this purpose as the liberty of the press, by which all the learning, wit, and the genius of the nation may be employed on the side of freedom, and every one be animated to its defense. As long, therefore, as the republican part of our government can maintain itself against the monarchical, it will naturally be careful to keep the press open, as of importance to its own preservation.—*Hume.*[94]

---

[93] From "Herald of Freedom" (1844), though with the second and third stanzas exchanged.

[94] David Hume (1711-1776), Scottish philosopher. This passage is from his essay, "Of the Liberty of the Press."

Once to every man and nation comes the moment to decide,
In the strife of truth with Falsehood, for the good or evil side;
Some great cause, God's new Messiah, offering each the bloom or
    blight,
Parts the goats upon the left hand, and the sheep upon the right,
And the choice goes by forever 'twixt that darkness and that light.[95]
New occasions teach new duties; Time makes ancient good uncouth;
They must upward still, and onward, who keep abreast of Truth;
Lo, before us gleam her camp-fires! we ourselves must Pilgrims be,
Launch our Mayflower and steer boldly through the desperate
    winter sea,
Nor attempt the Future's portal with the Past's blood-rusted key.[96]
—*James Russell Lowell.*

◊

When for the free human beings of the future it will no longer be the purpose of life to obtain the means of subsistence, but, as a result of a new belief, or rather knowledge, they will be certain of obtaining the means of subsistence in return for an appropriate natural activity, when in short, industry will no longer be our mistress, but our servant, the true purpose of life will become the enjoyment of life, and by education we will endeavor to make our children capable of its real enjoyment. An education, founded on the exercise of strength and the care of physical beauty, will, owing to the love for the child and the joy at the development of its beauty, become a purely artistic one, and every human being will in some way be a true artist. The diversity of natural inclinations will develop the most manifold tendencies in an unthought-of wealth.—*Richard Wagner.*[97]

◊

"Educate women like men," says Rousseau, "and the more they resemble our sex the less power will they have over us." This is the very point I aim at. I

---

[95] From "Once to Every Man and Nation," written in December 1845, in opposition to America's war with Mexico.
[96] From "The Present Crisis."
[97] Richard Wagner (1813-1883), German opera composer. From his 1849 essay, "Art and Revolution."

do not wish them to have power over men, but over themselves. [...] It is not empire, but equality and friendship, which women want. [...] Speaking of women at large, their first duty is to themselves as rational creatures, and the next, in point of importance, as citizens. [...]

Men submit everywhere to oppression, when they have only to lift their heads to throw off the yoke; yet, instead of asserting their birthright, they quietly lick the dust and say, Let us eat and drink, for tomorrow we die. Women, I argue from analogy, are degraded by the same propensity to enjoy the present moment; and, at last, despise the freedom which they have not sufficient virtue to struggle to attain.—*Mary Wollstonecraft*.[98]

◊

I think the religious tests were invented not so much to secure religion as the emoluments of it. When a religion is good, I conceive that it will support itself; and when it does not support itself, and God does not take care to support it, so that its professors are obliged to call for help of the civil power, 'tis a sign, I apprehend, of its being a bad one.

If we look back into history for the character of the present sects in Christianity, we shall find few that have not in their turns been persecutors, and complainers of persecution. The primitive Christians thought persecution extremely wrong in the Pagans, but practiced it on one another. The first Protestants of the Church of England blamed persecution in the Romish church, but practiced it upon the Puritans. These found it wrong in the Bishops, but fell into the same practice themselves both here (England) and in New England. —*Benjamin Franklin*.[99]

◊

Every new truth which has ever been propounded has, for a time, caused mischief; it has produced discomfort, and often unhappiness; sometimes by disturbing social or religious arrangements, and sometimes merely by the

---

[98] Mary Wollstonecraft (1759-1797), English writer and early feminist. She wrote *A Vindication of the Rights of Woman* (1792), scattered excerpts of which were cobbled together to form this passage.

[99] The first paragraph is from Franklin's 9 October 1780 letter to Richard Price. The second paragraph is from a 3 June 1772 letter to the *London Packet*, signed "A New-England-Man."

disruption of old and cherished association of thoughts. It is only after a certain interval, and when the frame-work of affairs has adjusted itself to the new truth, that its good effects preponderate; and the preponderance continues to increase, until, at length, the truth causes nothing but good. But, at the outset there is always harm. And if the truth is very great as well as very new the harm is serious. Men are made uneasy; they flinch; they cannot bear the sudden light; a general restlessness supervenes; the face of society is disturbed, or perhaps convulsed; old interests and old beliefs have been destroyed before new ones have been created. These symptoms are the precursors of revolution; they have preceded all the great changes through which the world has passed.—*Buckle's "History of Civilization."*[100]

◊

We do not mean merely freedom from restraint or compulsion. We do not mean merely freedom to do as we like, irrespectively of what it is that we like. We do not mean a freedom that can be enjoyed by one man or one set of men at the cost of a loss of freedom to others. When we speak of freedom as something to be highly prized, we mean a positive power or capacity of doing or enjoying something worth doing or enjoying, and that, too, something that we do or enjoy in common with others. We mean by it a power which each man exercises through the help or security given him by his fellowmen, and which he in turn helps to secure for them. When we measure the progress of a society by the growth in freedom, we measure it by the increasing development and exercise on the whole of those powers of contributing to social good with which we believe the members of the society to be endowed; in short, by the greater power on the part of the citizens as a body to make the most and best of themselves. —*Prof. T. H. Green.*[101]

---

[100] Henry Thomas Buckle (1821-1862), English historian. *His History of Civilization in England,* planned for fourteen volumes, was never completed. This quotation is from volume four.

[101] Thomas Hill Green (1836-1882), English political philosopher. The above lines are from a lecture, "On Liberal Legislation and Freedom of Contract" (1880).

There is only one cure for evils which newly-acquired freedom produces, and that cure is freedom. When a prisoner first leaves his cell, he cannot bear the light of day, he is unable to discriminate colors, or recognize faces. The remedy is, to accustom him to the rays of the sun.

The blaze of truth and liberty may at first dazzle and bewilder nations which have become half blind in the house of bondage. But let them gaze on, and they will soon be able to bear it. In a few years men learn to reason. The extreme violence of opinions subsides. Hostile theories correct each other. The scattered elements of truth cease to contend, and begin to coalesce. And, at length, a system of justice and order is educed out of the chaos.

Many politicians of our time are in the habit of laying it down as a self-evident proposition, that no people ought to be free till they are fit to use their freedom. The maxim is worthy of the fool in the old story, who resolved not to go into the water till he had learned to swim. If men are to wait for liberty till they become wise and good in slavery, they may indeed wait forever.—*Macaulay*.[102]

◊

Indeed, no opinion or doctrine, of whatever nature it be, or whatever be its tendency, ought to be suppressed. For it is either manifestly true, or it is manifestly false, or its truth or falsehood is dubious. Its tendency is manifestly good, or manifestly bad, or it is dubious and concealed. There are no other assignable conditions, no other functions of the problem.

In the case of its being manifestly true, and of good tendency, there can be no dispute. Nor in the case of its being manifestly otherwise; for by the terms it can mislead nobody. If its truth or its tendency be dubious, it is clear that nothing can bring the good to light, or expose the evil, but full and free discussion. Until this takes place, a plausible fallacy may do harm; but discussion is sure to elicit the truth, and fix public opinion on a proper basis; and nothing else can do it. […]

Criminality can only be predicated where there is an obstinate, unreasonable refusal to consider any kind of evidence but what exclusively supports one side of a question. […]

---

[102] Thomas Babington Macaulay (1800-1859), British historian and politician. His *History of England from the Accession of James the Second*, is a prime example of "Whig interpretation history," the portrayal of history as a glorious unfolding, of an inevitable progression toward an enlightened present. The quotation above is from Macaulay's essay, "Milton," published in the *Edinburgh Review* in 1825.

It follows that errors of the understanding must be treated by appeals to the understanding. That argument should be opposed by argument, and fact by fact. That fine and imprisonment are bad forms of syllogism, well calculated to irritate, but powerless for refutation. They may suppress truth, they can never elicit it. —*Thomas Cooper.*[103]

◊

If I could have entertained the slightest apprehension that the Constitution framed in the Convention when I had the honor to preside, might possibly endanger the religious rights of any ecclesiastical society, certainly I would never have placed my signature to it; and if I could now conceive that the general government might be so administered as to render the liberty of conscience insecure, I beg you will be persuaded that no one would be more zealous than myself to establish effectual barriers against the horrors of spiritual tyranny and every species of religious persecution.

[....] Of all the animosities which have existed among mankind, those which are caused by a difference of sentiments in religion appear to be the most inveterate and distressing, and ought most to be deprecated. I was in hopes that the enlightened and liberal policy, which has marked the present age, would at least have reconciled Christians of every denomination so far that we should never again see their religious disputes carried to such a pitch as to endanger the peace of society.

[....] Government is not reason, it is not eloquence—it is force! Like fire it is a dangerous servant and a fearful master; never for a moment should it be left to irresponsible action.

[....] The government of the United States of America is not, in any sense, founded upon the Christian religion.—*George Washington.*[104]

---

[103] Thomas Cooper (1759-1839), British political philosopher, economist and chemist, who later moved to the United States and became a president of South Carolina College (now University of South Carolina). The quotation assembles lines from different parts of Cooper's Treatise on the *Law of Libel and the Liberty of the Press* (1830).

[104] George Washington (1732-1799), American general and statesman. The first paragraph is from a May 1789 letter to the United Baptist Churches of Virginia. The second is from a 20 October 1792 letter to Sir Edward Newenham. The third quote ("Government is not reason...") is spurious, with no occurrence of these lines found before 1902. The final paragraph is not by Washington, but is from Article 11 of the Treaty of Tripoli, signed by President John Adams in 1796.

THE SOLDIER'S CREED

"Captain, what do you think," I asked,

"Of the part your soldiers play?"

But the captain answered, "I do not think;

I do not think, I obey!"

"Do you think you should shoot a patriot down, Or help a tyrant
       slay?"

But the captain answered, "I do not think;

I do not think, I obey!"

"Do you think your conscience was made to die,

And your brain to rot away?"

But the captain answered, "I do not think;

I do not think, I obey!"

"Then if this is your soldier's creed," I cried,

"You're a mean unmanly crew;

And for all your feathers and gilt and braid

I am more of a man than you!

"For whatever my place in life may be,

And whether I swim or sink,

I can say with pride, 'I do not obey;

I do not obey, I think!'"

—*Ernest Crosby*[105]

---

[105] Ernest Howard Crosby (1856-1907), American politician, Georgist, poet, friend of Leo Tostoy. This poem appears with the title "The Military Creed" in Crosby's 1902 book of verse, S*words and Ploughshares,* where a prefatory remark reads: "The American Admiral in command at Samoa was asked what he thought of expansion. He is reported to have answered, 'I do not think; I obey orders.'"

NO MASTER

Saith man to man, We've heard and known
That we no master need
To live upon this earth, our own,
In the fair and manly deed;
The grief of slaves long passed away
For us hath forged the chain,
Till now each worker's patient day
Builds up the House of Pain.
And we, shall we too crouch and quail,
Ashamed, afraid of strife;
And lest our lives untimely fail,
Embrace the death in life?
Nay, cry aloud and have no fear;
We few against the world;
Awake, arise! the hope we bear
Against the curse is hurl'd.
It grows, it grows: are we the same,
The feeble band, the few?
Or what are these with eyes aflame,
And hands to deal and do?
This is the host that bears the word,
No Master, High or Low,
A lightning flame, a shearing sword,
A storm to overthrow.
—*William Morris*[106]

---

[106] William Morris (1834-1896), British medievalist, poet, revolutionary socialist.

Let us all labor to add all needful guarantees for the more perfect security of free thought, free speech, and free press, pure morals, unfettered religious sentiments, and of equal rights and privileges to all men, irrespective of nationality, color, or religion. Encourage free schools, and resolve that not one dollar of money shall be appropriated to the support of any sectarian school. Resolve that neither the state nor nation, or both combined, shall support institutions of learning other than those sufficient to afford every child growing up in the land the opportunity of a good common school education, unmixed with sectarian, pagan, or atheistical tenets. Leave the matter of religion to the family altar, the church, and the private schools, supported entirely by private contributions. Keep the church and the state forever separate.

[....] I would call your attention to the importance of correcting an evil that, if permitted to continue, will probably lead to great trouble in our land before the close of the nineteenth century. It is the acquisition of vast amounts of untaxed church property. In 1850, I believe, the church property of the United States, which paid no tax, municipal or state, amounted to about $83,000,000. In 1860 the amount had doubled. In 1875 it is about $1,000,000,000. By 1900, without check, it is safe to say this property will reach a sum exceeding $3,000,000,000. So vast a sum, receiving all the protection and benefits of government without bearing its proportion of the burdens and expenses of the same, will not be looked upon acquiescently by those who have to pay the taxes. In a growing country, where real estate enhances so rapidly with time as in the United States, there is scarcely a limit to the wealth that may be acquired by corporations, religious or otherwise, if allowed to retain real estate without taxation. The contemplation of so vast a property as here alluded to, without taxation, may lead to sequestration without constitutional authority, and through blood. I would suggest the taxation of all property equally, whether church or corporation.—*U. S. Grant.*[107]

---

[107] Ulysses S. Grant (1822-1885), American general and politician. The first paragraph is from a 29 September 1875 address at an Army of the Tennessee reunion in Des Moines, Iowa. The passage following comes from his State of the Union Address, 7 December 1875. These nativist, anti-Catholic sentiments led to the Blaine Amendment, prohibiting use of government funds for sectarian schools. Although it failed at the federal level, similar language was adopted by most states,

In a word, there is scarcely a disposition that marks the love of abstract truth and scarcely a rule which reason teaches as essential for its attainment, that theologians did not, for centuries, stigmatize as offensive to the Almighty. By destroying every book that could generate discussion, by diffusing through every field of knowledge a spirit of boundless credulity, and, above all, by persecuting with atrocious cruelty those who differed from their opinions, they succeeded for a long period in almost arresting the action of the European mind, and in persuading men that a critical, impartial, and enquiring spirit was the worst form of vice. From this frightful condition Europe was at last rescued by the intellectual influences that produced the Reformation, by the teaching of those great philosophers who clearly laid down the conditions of enquiry, and by those bold innovators who, with the stake of Bruno[108] and Vanini[109] before their eyes, dared to challenge directly the doctrines of the past. By those means the spirit of philosophy or of truth became prominent, and the spirit of dogmatism, with all its consequences, was proportionately weakened. As long as the latter spirit possessed an indisputable ascendency, persecution was ruthless, universal, and unquestioned. When the former spirit became more powerful, the language of anathema grew less peremptory. Exceptions and qualifications were introduced; the full meaning of the words was no longer realized; persecution became languid; it changed its character; it exhibited itself rather in a general tendency than in overt acts; it grew apologetical, timid and evasive. In one age the persecutor burnt the heretic; in another, he crushed him with penal laws; in a third, he withheld from him places of emolument and dignity; in a fourth, he subjected him to the excommunication of society. Each stage of advancing toleration marks a stage of the decline of the spirit of dogmatism and of the increase of the spirit of truth.

[...] On the other hand, men who have been deeply imbued with the spirit of earnest and impartial enquiry, will invariably come to value such a disposition

---

[108] Giordano Bruno (1548-1600) was a Dominican friar who was burned at the stake by the Inquisition in Rome for his heretical cosmological theories.

[109] Lucilio Vanini (1585-1619), Italian philosopher and physician. Like Bruno, he was found guilty of having odd ideas. For this crime his tongue was cut out, he was strangled, and then, as an extra precaution, his body was burned.

more than any particular doctrines to which it may lead them; they will deny
the necessity of correct opinions; they will place the moral far above the dog-
matic side of their faith; they will give free scope to every criticism that restricts
their belief; and they will value men according to their acts, and not at all
according to their opinions. The first of these tendencies is essentially Roman
Catholic. The second is essentially rationalistic.—*W.E.H. Lecky.* [110]

◊

The greatest thing in the world is for a man to know that he is his own. [...]

We ought to hold with all our force, both of hands and teeth, the use of the
pleasures of life that one after another our years snatch away from us. [...]

To speak less of one's self than what one really is, is folly, not modesty; and
to take that for current pay which is under a man's value is pusillanimity and
cowardice. [...]

Retire yourself into yourself, but first prepare yourself there to receive yourself;
it were folly to trust yourself in your own hands if you cannot govern yourself.
[...]

We have lived long enough for others; let us, at least, live out the small remnant
of life for ourselves; let us now call in our thoughts and intentions to ourselves.
[...]

It is a wretched and dangerous thing to depend upon others; we ourselves, in
whom is ever the most just and safest dependence, are not sufficiently sure. I
have nothing mine but myself. [...]

It is not enough to get remote from the public; 'tis not enough to shift the soil
only; a man must flee from the popular conditions that have taken possession
of his soul, he must sequester and come again to himself. [...]

My trade and art is to live; he that forbids me to speak according to my own
sense, experience and practice, may as well enjoin an architect not to speak of
building according to his own knowledge, but according to that of his neighbor;
according to the knowledge of another and not according to his own. [...]

---

[110] William Edward Hartpole Lecky (1838-1903), Irish author and historian. The quotation is from his *History of the Rise and Influence of the Spirit of Rationalism in Europe*
(1865).

As for the fine saying, with which ambition and avarice palliate their vices, that
we are not born for ourselves but for the public, let us boldly appeal to those
who are in public affairs; let them lay their hands upon their hearts and then
say whether, on the contrary, they do rather aspire to titles and offices and that
tumult of the world to make their private advantage at the public expense. [...]

The laws keep up their credit, not by being just, but because they are laws;
'tis the mystic foundation of their authority; they have no other, and it well
answers their purpose. They are often made by fools; still oftener by men who,
out of hatred to equality, fail in equity; but always by men, vain and irresolute
authors. There is nothing so.much, nor so grossly, nor so ordinarily faulty, as
the laws. Whoever obeys them because they are just, does not justly obey them
as he ought.—*Montaigne.*[111]

◊

Where there is but one there is neither liberty nor slavery. Where there are
more than one there may be despotism (sometimes called "government,"
sometimes "absolute liberty") for one or more, and liberty for one or more, or
there may be approximate equal liberty for all.

In a word, the conception and the facts of liberty and slavery result from association, not isolation; and the sparseness or density of population, the simplicity
or complexity of association, will create the customs, rules and laws governing
human relations. Therefore, what the solitary man rightfully may do is no measure of what he rightfully may do when he comes into contact with another
man. The liberty of one is conditioned by the liberty of the other.

Thomas Paine wrote these words in The Crisis: "The Grecians and the Romans
were strongly possessed of the spirit of liberty but not the principle, for at the
time they were determined not to be slaves themselves, they employed their
power to enslave the rest of mankind."

...The kind of equal liberty possible is determined by environment. It is not
a matter of guesswork, of intuition; it is not indicated by the undisciplined

---

[111] Michel Eyquem de Montaigne (1533-1592), French Renaissance philosopher,
famous for his three books of short literary essays. The above passages were assembled
from excerpts of four essays: "Of Solitude," "Use Makes Perfect," "Of Vanity" and "Of
Experience."

spirit of mastership which sometimes expresses itself today in the demand for
"absolute" freedom. It is to be ascertained by the activities of brain and tested by
ethics, ethics here meaning the conception of fair play, of the nearest possible
equality of opportunity. For equal liberty simply means fair play.

Of course "equal liberty" does not mean equal liberty to invade, to indulge in
"self-expression" careless of the thus denied self-expression of others, to rob, to
tyrannize, as careless or unbalanced thinkers sometimes have said, but equal
freedom from invasion, from robbery, from the exaction of tyranny. Fair play
(liberty) cannot exist in the atmosphere of absolutism, whether the absolutism
be that of czar, majority, or lawless individual outside of formal government.
—*Edwin C. Walker.*[112]

◊

In all ages, the truest lovers of mankind have toiled to imbue their fellows
with the spirit of open-mindedness. The cause of free-speech numbers the
most glorious martyrs in history, Socrates, whose name we hold in reverence
today, was murdered by the Athenian people, for seeking to lead them to
think for themselves. Bruno in death and Galileo in imprisonment paid the
penalty of loving truth more than public opinion. Roger Bacon upheld the
cause of scientific research against unnumbered persecutions. Milton per-
ceived that no error was so fatal as the suppression of thought, and penned
his glorious *Areopagitica*,[113] which remains to this day an unanswerable argument to all who, either from mental weakness or from a tyrannous disposition, seek to set bounds to human speculation or expression. Voltaire, Paine
and a host of others have followed in demonstrating that free minds and free
lips were necessary, in order that men might grow and learn. In our own land,
Elijah Lovejoy[114] gave his life for the principle of freedom of the press; and

---

[112] Edwin C. Walker (1849-1931), American individualist anarchist. This quotation is
from his 1913 pamphlet, *The Ethics of Freedom.*
[113] John Milton's 1644 published "speech" (it was never actually delivered but was
written in the form of a speech) defending freedom of expression and speech. It was
immensely influential and provides insights even when read today, 375 years later.
[114] Elijah Parish Lovejoy (1802-1837), American Presbyterian minister, journalist and
abolitionist martyr. He was killed by a pro-slavery mob in Alton, Illinois in 1837.

from his martyrdom was born the grand apostleship of Wendell Phillips[115] in the cause of freedom. We stand indeed on holy ground, when we approach the sublime company of those who, through the ages, have striven to secure, not only for themselves, but for all mankind, the right of unfettered utterance on every theme. Well for us, if we are found worthy to tread in their footsteps, and to bear the most humble part in this great work.—*James F. Morton.*[116]

◊

The philosophy of Egoism, which is merely the doctrine of evolution applied to psychology, teaches us that each individual always seeks his own greatest happiness. Any interference with an individual in the pursuit of his happiness is unwarranted, as no one can know better than the person himself in what direction his happiness lies. Individual freedom is necessary to the attainment of individual happiness. Any restraint of the free activities of the individual are [sic] certain to violate the conditions of social progress. [...]

If freedom is the condition of progress, all invasion of that freedom is bad and should be resisted, whether it is practiced by one upon another, by one upon many, or by many upon one. In other words, individual freedom presupposes the suppression of the invader, whether that invader appears as an individual criminal or as the corporate criminal—the State,—and whether as the Republican or as the Imperial form of State. [...]

The first essentials of freedom are, of course, the freedom to live unmolested and the freedom of the producer to retain unrestricted the full product of his toil. While there may be serious differences of opinion in regard to the definitions of "producer" and "product," I think no one will deny that crimes against person and property—murder, assault, theft, etc.—are violations of Equal Freedom.—*Francis D. Tandy.*[117]

---

[115] Wendell Phillips (1811-1884), American attorney, leading abolitionist. For his eloquence he was called, "Abolition's Golden Trumpet."

[116] James Ferdinand Morton, Jr. (1870-1941), American individualist anarchist. The quotation most likely comes from his 1900 pamphlet, *Do You Want Free Speech?*, though this has not been verified.

[117] Francis Dashwood Tandy (1867-1913), American mutualism/voluntaryist. The passage was assembled from excerpts from Tandy's book *Voluntary Socialism: A Sketch* (1896).

No man ever ruled other men for their own good; no man was ever rightly the master of the minds or bodies of his brothers; no man ever ruled other men for anything except for their undoing and for his own brutalization. The possession of power over others is inherently destructive both to the possessor of the power and to those over whom it is exercised. And the great man of the future, in distinction from the great man of the past, is he who will seek to create power in the people, and not gain power over them. The great man of the future is he who will refuse to be great at all, in the historic sense; he is the man who will literally lose himself, who will altogether diffuse himself, in the life of humanity. All that any man can do for a people, all, that any man can do for another man, is to set the man or the people free. Our work, whensoever and wheresoever we would do good, is to open to men the gates of life—to lift up the heavenly doors of opportunity. [...]

Give men opportunity and opportunity will give you men.—*George D. Herron*.[118]

◊

It is the fundamental condition of liberty that no one shall be deprived of the opportunity of securing the full product of his labor. Economic independence is consequently the first demand of Anarchism; the abolition of the exploitation of man by man. That exploitation is made impossible: by the freedom of banking, i.e. liberty in the matter of furnishing a medium of exchange free from the legal burden of interest; by the freedom of credit, i.e. the organization of credit on the basis of the principle of mutualism, of economic solidarity; by the freedom of home and foreign trade, i.e. liberty of unhindered exchange of values from hand to hand as from land to land; the freedom of land, i. e. liberty in the occupation of land for the purpose of personal use, if it is not already occupied by others for the same purpose; or, to epitomize all these demands: the exploitation of man by man is made impossible by the freedom of labor.—*John Henry Mackay*.[119]

---

[118] George D. Herron (1862-1925), an American clergyman and socialist, member of the "Social Gospel" movement. The above passage is from Herron's essay, "Theodore Roosevelt," published in the June 1910 issue of *The International Socialist Review*.

[119] John Henry Mackay (1864-1933), Scottish-born anarchist who lived in Berlin. The above passage is from his *The Anarchists: A Picture of Civilization at the Close of the Nineteenth Century* (1891).

I have lived with communities of savages in South America and in the East, who have no laws or law-courts but the public opinion of the village freely expressed. Each man scrupulously respects the rights of his fellow, and any infraction of those rights rarely or never takes place. In such a community all are nearly equal. There are none of those wide distinctions of education and ignorance, wealth and poverty, master and servant, which are the production of our civilization. There is none of that wide-spread division of labor, which, while it increases wealth, produces also conflicting interests. There is not that severe competition and struggle for existence or for wealth which the dense population of civilized countries inevitably creates. All incitements to great crimes are thus wanting, and petty ones are suppressed partly by the influence of public opinion, but chiefly by that natural sense of justice and his neighbor's right which seem to be in some degree inherent in every race of men.—*Alfred Russell Wallace.*[120]

◊

Liberty is the most jealous and exacting mistress that can beguile the brain and soul of man. From him who will not give her all, she will have nothing. She knows that his pretended love serves but to betray. But when once the fierce heat of her quenchless, lustrous eyes has burned into the victim's heart, he will know no other smile but hers. Liberty will have none but the great devoted souls, and by her glorious visions, by her lavish promises, her boundless hopes, her infinitely witching charms, she lures these victims over hard and stony ways, by desolate and dangerous paths, through misery, obloquy and want to a martyr's cruel death. Today we pay our last sad homage to the most devoted lover, the most abject slave, the fondest, wildest, dreamiest victim that ever gave his life to liberty's immortal cause. —*Clarence S. Darrow, at Altgeldt's funeral.*[121]

---

[120] Alfred Russell Wallace (1823-1913), British naturalist and explorer, from his *The Malay Archipelago: The Land of the Orang-Utan, and the Bird of Paradise. A Narrative of Travel, with Studies of Man and Nature* (1869).

[121] Clarence Seward Darrow (1857-1938), American labor lawyer and civil libertarian. Spencer Tracy played him in the 1960 film, *Inherit the Wind*, which covered the famous Scopes Monkey Trial. The subject of the funeral address, John Peter Altgeld, worked in Darrow's law office after retiring from politics. The funeral address (14 March 1902) was reprinted in an appendix to Darrow's autobiography, *The Story of My Life.*

To be governed, is to be watched, inspected, spied, directed, law-ridden, regulated, penned up, indoctrinated, preached at, checked, appraised, seized, censured, commanded, by beings who have neither title nor knowledge nor virtue. To be governed is to have every operation, every transaction, every movement noted, registered, counted, rated, stamped, measured, numbered, assessed, licensed, refused, authorized, indorsed, admonished, prevented, reformed, redressed, corrected. To be governed is, under pretext of public utility and in the name of the general interest, to be laid under contribution, drilled, fleeced, exploited, monopolized, extorted from, exhausted, hoaxed and robbed; then, upon the slightest resistance, at the first word of complaint, to be repressed, fined, vilified, annoyed, hunted down, pulled about, beaten, disarmed, bound, imprisoned, shot, mitrailleused,[122] judged, condemned, banished, sacrificed, sold, betrayed, and, to crown all, ridiculed, derided, outraged, dishonored.—*Proudhon.*[123]

◊

Every attempt to gag the free expression of thought is an unsocial act, a crime against society. That is why judges and juries who try to enforce these laws make themselves ridiculous. It is very hard for a robber to convince his victims that he is acting in their behalf and for their good. Is there no parallel between the gag of the burglar and the gag of the law? Why does the burglar use a gag? It is because he wants to get away with your goods, and he doesn't want you to make an outcry and call the neighbors. He knows that he cannot convince you by argument that he is entitled to the goods and that it is really to your best interest to pass them over to him. Capitalism holds up the toilers; it robs them of their labor and is enjoying life to its fullest on the result of its plunder. Naturally it doesn't want to be deprived of its special privilege, therefore it puts the gag of the law in the mouth of anyone who attempts to make an outcry.—*Jay Fox.*[124]

---

[122] The original French text uses here the term *mitraillé* which is being hit with grape-shot. It appears that some later translator "upgraded" the verb to *mitrailleuse*, shot with a volley gun, perhaps due to its notoriety from being used to execute members of the Paris Commune in 1871..

[123] Pierre-Joseph Proudhon (1809-1865), French mutualist/anarchist. Nozick (in *Anarchy, State, and Utopia*) traces this quotation to John Beverly Robinson's 1923 translation of Proudhon's *General Idea of the Revolution in the Nineteenth Century* (1851), though obviously Sprading must have had access to another, earlier English translation, or the original, since Sprading published the above in 1913.

[124] Jay Fox (1870-1961), American anarchist, communist, labor activist. No definitive original source for this passage has been found, but it was widespread in socialist publications in the early 20th century, e.g., *The Commonwealth* (Everett, Washington), 30 October 1913.

Make no laws whatever concerning speech, and speech will be free; so soon as you make a declaration on paper that speech shall be free, you will have a hundred lawyers proving that "freedom does not mean abuse, nor liberty license;" and they will define and define freedom out of existence. Let the guarantee of free speech be in every man's determination to use it, and we shall have no need of paper declarations. On the other hand, so long as the people do not care to exercise their freedom, those who wish to tyrannize will do so; for tyrants are active and ardent, and will devote themselves in the name of any number of gods, religious and otherwise, to put shackles upon sleeping men.—*Voltairine De Cleyre.*[125]

◊

Of course if we knew the whole truth Liberty would not be so necessary as far as the race is concerned. But because we do not know the truth we must leave all the avenues for its discovery open, and hence every individual must have perfect liberty to follow his own inclination and desire. In this way all of society would be transformed into one great sociological laboratory in which all the isms in each succeeding age would be subjected to laboratory tests and only the truths remain. Not only does Liberty solve all of our sociological problems but it is the only possible source for material advancement. The innumerable social advantages that have come from individual inventions and discoveries illustrate this. Thus it must be perfectly plain that if the race is to climb to higher levels and make still farther advances the one big prime necessity for such advancement is Liberty.—*Dr. Claude Riddle.*[126]

◊

Instead of defending "free love," which is a much-abused term capable of many interpretations, we ought to strive for the freedom of love; for while the former has come to imply freedom for any sort of love, the latter must only mean freedom for a feeling which is worthy the name of love. This

---

[125] Voltairine De Cleyre (1866-1912), an American free-thinker and proponent of "anarchism without adjectives." In 2018 the *New York Times* published a belated obituary, calling her "America's Greatest Woman Anarchist." Her essay, "Anarchism and American Traditions" is the source of the above quotation.

[126] Claude Riddle (?-?), American socialist, labor activist in Los Angeles, president of the local Industrial Workers of the World (the "Wobblies"). No source for the above quotation has been located.

feeling, it may be hoped, will gradually win for itself the same freedom in life as it already possesses in poetry. The flowering, as well as the budding of love, will then be a secret between the lovers, and only its fruits will be a matter between them and society. As always, poetry has pointed out the way to development. A great poet has seldom sung of lawfully wedded happiness, but often of free and secret love; and in this respect, too, the time is coming when there will no longer be one standard of morality for poetry and another for life. To anyone tender of conscience, the ties formed by a free connection are stronger than the legal ones, since in the former case he has made a choice more decisive to his own and the other's personality than if he had followed law and custom.—*Ellen Key.*[127]

◊

God so made us, and put such instincts in us, that to gratify them is wrong, and to crush them is right; to be happy is wicked, while to be miserable is righteousness. The old asceticism said: "Be virtuous, and you will be happy." The new hedonism says: "Be happy and you will be virtuous." Self-development is greater than self-sacrifice. It will make each in the end more helpful to humanity. To be sound in mind and limb; to be healthy of body and mind; to be educated, to be emancipated, to be free, to be beautiful,—these things are ends towards which all should strain, and by attaining which all are happier in themselves, and more useful to others. That is the central idea of the new hedonism.—*Grant Allen.*[128]

◊

Men mistake when they imagine the Single Tax agitation to aim only at fiscal change, a new method of taxation. Its sole purpose is to secure the larger freedom of the race. It is not the method but the result that is precious. For it is idle to talk of the equal rights of men when the one thing essential to such equality is withheld. The Physiocrats of France grasped the central truth, and saw that freedom of natural opportunity, comprised in the term land, was the foundation-stone of freedom and justice. Had the French Revolution

---

[127] Ellen Key (1849-1926), a Swedish feminist, author of *Love and Marriage,* from which this quotation was taken.
[128] Grant Allen (18481-1899), Canadian writer. His essay, "The New Hedonism" (1900), provided the above passage.

proceeded on their line, it would have had a different ending. The succeeding spectre of Napoleon, devastating Europe and wading through the blood of his sacrificed countrymen to the throne, would not have affrighted mankind. The fruits of liberty would have been gathered.—*William Lloyd Garrison.*[129]

◊

It is vain to echo Nietzsche's mad cry for absolute freedom—the freedom of the strong to enslave the weak, of the cunning to rob the candid. That we already have and it does not satisfy. The personal life cannot satisfy the growing sympathies of man. The demand of the centuries, never so virile and insistent as today, is for equal freedom. The modern Everyman asks not for himself what all may not have. The asking were vain, indeed, for there is no freedom till all are free. Master and slave are bound by the same thong. Human solidarity is not a moral fancy but a stern fact. —*Luke North (Editor of Everyman).*[130]

◊

The Single Tax does not intend to add to or multiply the already almost infinite statutory enactments now confusing and befuddling the social state, but rather means to abolish, one after the other, every law on the statute books granting a special privilege to any one man or body of men that is at the expense of the unprivileged mass of society. This will destroy the petty and grand larceny now preying upon the social body.

Aside from the million of petty privileges granted by municipalities, states and the nation to individuals, the great and glorious pillage shows itself in privileges and monopoly in laborsaving inventions, trade restrictions and the private ownership of natural resources, the major part of which is a matter of taxation; therefore, the Single Tax would abolish all taxes on barter, trade, exchange, personal property and improvements, commensurately raising all taxes from the value of land alone, till there was in existence but one single tax upon the

---

[129] William Lloyd Garrison, Jr. (1838-1909), American social reformer, advocate of the single tax, son of a famous abolitionist leader. This is from a speech Garrison delivered in San Francisco, 27 April 1903.

[130] Luke North (?-?), American single-tax proponent, editor of *Everyman*, published irregularly by the Single Tax League of Los Angeles from 1906-1919. No issues of this magazine have been located, the possible source of this quotation.

value of bare land exclusive of improvements. This would be a single tax on land value—not on land, for some land would pay no tax while other land would pay much tax.

For instance, one acre of land worth a million dollars would pay as much tax as a million acres worth only one dollar per acre.—*Edmund Norton*.[131]

◊

So long as society is founded on injustice, the function of the laws will be to defend and sustain injustice. And the more unjust they are, the more respectable they will seem. Observe also that, being ancient, for the most part, they do not represent altogether present iniquity, but a past iniquity—rougher and more brutal. They are the monuments of barbarous times which have survived to a gentler period.—*Anatole France*.[132]

◊

If that is the best government which governs least, is no government at all the summum bonum? What use for Church or State if man, with every burden cast off, every bond broken, rises to his full stature and development, with a spirit purified into selflessness by very surrender to the instincts of self! What is this but the sublimation, the apotheosis of Herbert Spencer's enlightened self-interest? What is it but Prof. James' Pragmatism[133]—the idea that there is no good but what is good to me?—*William Marion Reedy*.[134]

◊

The people, the stand-patters, who for profit, or for an unthinking but sincere conservatism, try to suppress radical tendencies because they fear revolution and destruction, are themselves fostering revolution and destruction.

---

[131] Edmund Norton (?-?), leader of the Georgean Single Tax League. The quotation is from a speech "What is the Single Tax?" given at the Jefferson Club, Los Angeles and published in the *Single Tax Review*, July-August 1910 issue.

[132] Anatole France (1844-1924), French novelist, recipient of the 1921 Nobel Prize in Literature. Although this passage was widely printed in trade union papers in the 1920s, no source of these lines in France's writings has yet been found.

[133] William James (1842-1910), Harvard professor, psychologist and philosopher, author of *Pragmatism*.

[134] William Marion Reedy (1862-1920), American editor and Georgist. He published a literary journal, *Reedy's Mirror*. These lines were reprinted in the December 1908 issue of *Mother Earth*, Emma Goldman's journal, under the title "The Daughter of the Dream," attributing it to Reedy in the *St. Louis Mirror*.

The force and power of their reactionary intolerance tend to make the idealist desperate and induce him to resort to violence; he, therefore, who stands in the way of free speech and free expression in art, politics or industry is an enemy of society.—*Hutchins Hapgood.*[135]

◊

This government was established to protect primarily the rights of men in social union, not the rights of property-holders, merely as such. Therefore, traffic in ideas is more important than traffic in merchandise. To suppress the former on pretense of protecting the latter, even in the use of streets, is an unpardonable outrage which becomes quite intolerable when done by arbitrary police violence, or with favoritism for approved opinions. —*Leonard Abbott.*[136]

◊

The political franchise for women is a strike in the direction of equal justice to all, regardless of sex, but woman has been endowed by nature with a franchise incomparably more important than any that man can bestow upon her, namely, the right to elect whether she shall become a mother or not, the right to elect her masculine helper in the creative process, and the added right to elect the economic conditions, the home surroundings under which she will consent to become a mother.—*Moses Harman.*[137]

◊

Noble souls wish not to have anything for nothing.

The crowd will follow a leader who marches twenty steps in advance; but if he is a thousand steps in front of them, they do not see and do not follow him, and any literary freebooter who chooses may shoot him with impunity. —*Georg Brandes.*[138]

---

[135] Hutchins Hapgood (1869-1944), American anarchist, journalist, drama critic, editorial writer. This passage is from his essay, "Fire and Revolution," published in the 11 July 1912 (N.Y.) *Globe*, and soon after issued as a pamphlet by the Free Speech League.

[136] Leonard Abbott (1878-1953), American radical, raised in England of American expatriate parents. In America he started as an anarchist and ended a socialist. The above passage appears to be from a pamphlet entitled, "Street Speaking."

[137] Moses Harman (1830-1910), American anarchist, publisher of the newsletter, *Lucifer the Lightbearer.* This passage is of unknown origin, but was attributed to "M.H." in the November-December 1908 issue of *The American Journal of Eugenics.*

[138] Georg Brandes (1842-1927), Danish literary critic. The passage quoted above was not political, but literary, referring to Shelly's poetry. It is from Brandes's *Naturalism in England* (1906).

It can never be unpatriotic for a man to take his country's side against his government; it must always be unpatriotic for a man to take his government's side against his country. —*Steven T. Byington*.[139]

◊

What is freedom? To have the will to be responsible for one's self. [...]

Whosoever will be free, must make himself free: freedom is no fairy's gift to fall into any man's lap.

Whatever the State saith is a lie; whatever it hath is a theft: all is counterfeit in it, the gnawing, sanguinary, insatiate monster. It even bites with stolen teeth. Its very bowels are counterfeit. [...]

We carry faithfully what we are given, on hard shoulders, over rough mountains! And when perspiring, we are told: "Yea, life is hard to bear!" But man himself only is hard to bear! The reason is that he carrieth too many strange things on his shoulders. Like the camel he kneeleth down and alloweth the heavy load to be put on his back.—*Nietzsche*.[140]

◊

More liberty, not less, is demanded by every rational thinker in the world today, but the clergy are not in that category, so we still see them sitting on the lid, so to speak, trying their best to keep liberty in check. [...]

Liberty to them is the most offensive word in the English language, and to keep the mass of mankind from enjoying it, has always been the prime object of priestcraft.—*Channing Severance*.[141]

◊

---

[139] Steven Tracy Byington (1869-1957), American individualist anarchist. No source for the quotation has been located, but it dates to at least 1903, when it was quoted in the 7 June 1903 issue of the free-thought newspaper, *Blue-Grass Blade* (Lexington, Kentucky).

[140] Friedrich Wilhelm Nietzsche (1844-1900), German philosopher. The above text was assembled from several texts, including *Twilight of the Idols* (first paragraph) and *Thus Spake Zarathustra* (the fourth paragraph). The source of the middle two paragraphs is unknown.

[141] Channing Severance (?-?), part of the Los Angeles liberal/anarchist/socialist society, an associate of Sprading. The above lines are from an essay published in *The Philistine*.

The glorification of the State as a kind of all-wise Providence has neither historic nor logical foundation. The quixotic belief of the Socialists that the State can be captured by the proletariat and used to expropriate the capitalists, then afterwards carry on all the industrial functions of society on collectivist principles, is as economically unsound as it is chimerical.—*William Bailie.*[142]

◊

Liberty, divinest word ever coined by human brain or uttered by human tongue. It is the spirit of liberty that today undermines the empires of the, old world, sets crowns and mitres askew, and in its onward elemental sweep is shaking the institutions of capitalism in this nation as frail weeds are shaken in the blasts of the storm king's fury.—*Eugene V. Debs.*[143]

◊

As for discussions about my one ideal form of government, they are simply idle.

The ideal form of government is no government at all.

The existence of government in any shape is a sign of man's imperfection. —*Professor E. A. Freeman.*[144]

Only a monopoly which prevented a free supply could for any length of time command tribute for the use of land, money, plant, or commodities. —*J. K. Ingalls.*[145]

◊

In general the art of government consists in taking as much money as possible from one part of the citizens to give it to another.—*Voltaire.*[146]

---

[142] William Bailie (?-?), American anarchist. These lines are from the introduction to his book, *Josiah Warren: The First American Anarchist* (1906).

[143] Eugene Victor Debs (1855-1926), American socialist, labor organizer, founder of the Wobblies. No original source for these lines has been found.

[144] Edward Augustus Freeman (1823-1892), English historian, artist, journalist and politician. This quotation is from his essay, "The Growth of Commonwealths," published in the reformist magazine, *The Fortnightly Review* (1 October 1873).

[145] Joshua King Ingalls (1816-1898), American land reformer whose *Economic Equities* (1887) is the source of the above quotation.

[146] From *Dictionnaire philosophique*, entry for "Argent" (money).

www.ingramcontent.com/pod-product-compliance
Lightning Source LLC
Chambersburg PA
CBHW030302030426
42336CB00009B/488